ADVANCE PRAISE FOR
*Eight Whopping Lies
and Other Stories of Bruised Grace*

Brian Doyle wrote more powerfully about faith than anyone in his generation. In the literary climate of the present time, to write about faith is a brave and original and contrary thing to do. Never didactic or overbearing, he showed us occurrences in life that burst with radiance—small epiphanies with enormous implications. And best of all, he could sneak up on you and really make you laugh. These are wonderful essays by a writer whose work will last and whose reputation will grow.

—Ian Frazier, author, *Great Plains* and
Lamentations of the Father

If a life can be said to be a collection of moments, then Brian Doyle's life is right here, glowing between the covers of this book. Each of these thirty-eight essays presents a little moment that, upon reflection, is everything but little. They are the memories and thoughts of a man who made it his purpose in life to recognize kindness, humor, grace, and beauty whenever he saw it. *Eight Whopping Lies* will make you a better person.

—Anthony Doerr, author, *All the Light We Cannot See*

Almost nobody has written with the joy, the galloping energy, the quiet love of conscience and family and what's best in us, the living optimism of Brian Doyle. He was one of the most generous and imaginative editors in America for decades, helping to fashion a magazine that was uniquely elegant and transformative. But he was also a writer—on faith and life and Van Morrison and fathers and sons and everything essential—it›s hard to imagine our seeing again. What a gift to have his beautiful and refulgent spirit with us again between the covers of a new book!

—Pico Iyer, author, *The Open Road* and *The Art of Stillness*

Brian Doyle's prose was lean and rhythmic while also being ornate in the way a branch is ornate when it's covered with green leaves. His poetry was that only moreso, beating like a bodhran, but his message was pretty much always the same. An examination of small moments. The search for what he called "grace." He also happens to be the best basketball writer I've ever read. Basketball exposed to me just how hard Brian could go, how determined he was. When I finally got to America in 2015, I found him walking with a limp. "Old basketball injury," he said with a grin. As a writer, as a man, I thought he was a brave, generous spirit. I thought of him as my American brother.

—Martin Flanagan, editor, *On Listening*

Eight Whopping Lies and Other Stories of Bruised Grace

Brian Doyle

franciscan
media
Cincinnati, Ohio

Cover and book design by Mark Sullivan

ISBN 978-1-63253-165-0

Published by Franciscan Media
28 W. Liberty St.
Cincinnati, OH 45202
www.FranciscanMedia.org

Printed in the United States of America.
Printed on acid-free paper.
17 18 19 20 21   5 4 3 2 1

To my friend John Roscoe,
with admiration for his quiet grace
and courage

Everything is held together with stories. That is all that is holding us together, stories and compassion.
—Barry Lopez

Contents

A Remembrance

By Jim Doyle, Brian's father

What a man! What a writer! What a great son, brother, husband and Dad!

Yes, Brian was hugely special for all of us—his mother Ethel and me, his sister Betsy and his brothers Kevin, Peter, and Tom, and their wives Jane, Sharon, and Diane, and our nine grandchildren. His love for his wife, Mary Miller, and their classy kids was one of his great joys. He told me often how much he loved Mary and their daughter Lily (whom he called "my little flower of the West") and their great twin sons, Joseph and Liam.

He also loved his fans, who cheered him for his exuberant writing and speaking. In his essays and poems, and in person, we learned his passion for God's creation—us marvelous human beings and the other creatures of our world—denizens of the woods, waters, and skies. He was surely one of America's best storytellers—a premier practitioner of the printed word, flaunting grammar rules while painting exquisite word pictures showing God's love for us.

Brian was a cheerful child—a friendly companion for his siblings and the rest of his growing-up community, watching out for his younger brothers, shooting baskets with Kevin and the gang, and with it all a good student, avid reader, and, even early on, an excellent writer. Some people may have thought he was a wild writer, uncontrolled, not paying attention to the rules, but that was not so. He was a hard worker and steady writer. He went to his university office early every day to write his own stuff, before others showed up, as well as during the days and weekends at home. The result was hundreds of hours of beautiful writing every year.

One time I found out he was doing a story about playing with a group of musicians on a tour of gigs in the mountains and I kidded him about it, suggesting he didn't have any great musical talent or knowledge. He told me confidentially that he'd been studying the music business, reading about it, talking to musicians and going to performances, so as to learn something about the business—just so he could write that one essay with authority. So there.

If he had been with us a few more years, his fame would certainly have grown and his name would have become very well-known in America and the reading world. But we family and fans were in time: We found him and enjoyed his talent and honored his creativity.

We are all enlightened by what Brian recognized and described—inspired by what he believed and told us about God's world and people. We are all the better, more holy, I believe, for all of that, and for Brian Doyle having been with us and among us.

Illuminos

One child held onto my left pinky finger everywhere we went. Never any other finger and never the right pinky but only the left pinky and never my whole hand. My finger misses her hand this morning. It has been many years since she held my finger. To this day sometimes in the morning when I dress I stare at my left pinky and suddenly I am in the playground, or on the beach, or in a thrumming crowd, and there is a person weighing forty pounds holding onto my left pinky so tightly that I am tacking slightly to port. I miss tacking slightly to port.

Another child held onto my left trouser leg most of the time but he would, if he deemed it necessary, hold either of my hands, and one time both of my hands, when we were shuffling in the surf, and the water was up to my knees but up to his waist, and I walked along towing him like a small grinning chortling dinghy all the way from the sea cave where we thought there might be sea lions sleeping off a salmon bender to the tide pools where you could find starfish and crabs and anemones and mussels the size of your shoes.

The third child held hands happily all the time, either hand, any hand, my hands, his mother's hands, his brother's hands, his sister's hands, his friends, aunts and uncles and cousins and grandparents and teachers, dogs and trees, neighbors and bushes, he would hold hands with any living creature whatsoever, without the slightest trepidation or self-conscious-ness, and to this day I admire that boy's open genuine eager unadorned verve. He once held hands with his best friend during an entire soccer game when they were five years old, the two of them running in tandem, or one starting in one direction unbeknownst to the other and down they both went giggling in the sprawl of the grass. It seems to me that angels and bodhisattvas are everywhere available for consultation if only we can see them clear; they are unadorned, and joyous, and patient, and radiant, and luminous, and not disguised or hidden or filtered in any way whatsoever, so that if you see them clearly, which happens occasionally even to the most blinkered and frightened of us, you realize immediately who they are, beings of great and humble illumination dressed in the skins of new and dewy beings, and you realize, with a catch in your throat, that they are your teachers, and they are agents of an unimaginable love, and they are your cousins and companions in awe, and they are miracles and prayers and songs of inexplicable beauty whom no one can explain and no one own or claim or trammel, and that simply to perceive them is to be blessed beyond the reach of language, and that to be the one appointed to tow them along a beach, or a crowd, or home through the brilliant morning from the muddy hilarious peewee soccer game, is to be graced beyond measure or understanding; which is what I was, and I am, and I will be, until the day I die, and change form from this one to another, in ways miraculous and mysterious, never to be plumbed by the mind or measures of man.

100th Street

By chance I was in New York City seven months after September 11, and I saw a moment that I still turn over and over in my mind like a puzzle, like a koan, like a prism.

I had spent the day at a conference crammed with uninformed opinions and droning speeches and stern lectures, and by the evening I was weary of it all, weary of being sermonized by pompous authority, weary of the cocksure and the arrogant and the tin-eared, weary of what sold itself as deeply religious but was actually grim moral policing with not the slightest hint of mercy or humility in the air, and I slipped out and away from the prescribed state dinner, which promised only more speeches and lectures.

I was way up on the upper west side of the Island of the Manhattoes, near the ephemeral border of Harlem, and as I was in the mood to walk off steam, I walked far and wide; down to the Sailors and Soldiers Monument, by the vast Hudson River, and up to Joan of Arc Park, with Joan on her rearing charger, and up to the Firemen's Memorial, on 100th Street. I thought about wandering up to the great old castle church of Saint John the Divine on 111th Street but by now I was footsore and yearning for beer and I stepped into a bar.

It was that russet hour between evening and night and the bar was populous but not crowded. Most of the people seemed to have stopped by for a beer after work. One table of men in the corner wore the faded coveralls of telephone linemen or public utility workers. Another table of mature women were in the bland dark uniforms of corporate staff. Interestingly there was a young Marine in glittering full dress uniform at the bar, with two older men I took to be his father and uncle, perhaps; they were laughing and resting their hands affectionately on his shoulders and he was smiling and savoring their hands like they were pet birds he had not had on his shoulders for a long time.

I got a beer and sat in the corner and watched as the bartender, who wore a lovely old-style long bowtie, set a beer in front of the Marine and waved off the uncle's offer to pay, and his little cheerful gesture made me happy, and I concluded that this would be the gentle tender respectful highlight of a day in which there had been very little respect and tenderness, but then the door opened, and two young firemen walked in. They were not in full dress uniform but they had their FDNY shirts on, and I noticed their sturdy work boots, and somehow you could tell that they were firemen and not just guys who happened to be wearing FDNY shirts.

They took a few steps toward the bar, and then something happened that I will never forget. Everyone in the bar stood up, silently. The table of women stood up first, I noticed, and then everyone else stood up, including me. I thought perhaps someone would start to applaud but no one made a sound. The men standing at the bar turned and faced the firemen, and then the young Marine drew himself up straight as a tree and saluted the firemen, and then his father and uncle saluted too, and then everyone else in the bar saluted the firemen. I tell you that there wasn't a sound in the place, not the clink of a glass or the shuffle of feet or a cough or anything.

After a few seconds one of the firemen nodded to everyone, and the other fireman made a slight gesture of acknowledgement with his right hand, and the bartender set two beers on the bar, and everyone sat down again, and everything went on as before; but not.

A Sprawl of Brothers

Sometimes we would all be sprawled on the floor, and for once there would be no grappling and wrassling, and we would be peaceful, with legs here and arms there and one brother using another for a pillow. If you lay flat you could imagine that you were surrounded by mountains and foothills of brothers, ridges and ranges of brothers, a burly wilderness of brothers. One would twitch and the others would rustle and shuffle and then we would recompose for a while. Maybe we were watching television or listening to the murmur of uncles. Our sister would stalk through like a heron sometimes, lifting her feet gingerly. Sometimes you would doze off for a few minutes and startle awake and everything was the same except for the conversation overhead. Their legs were like logs and their arms were like branches. Here and there you could see a grumble of hair. Somewhere in the pile there might be a cousin. Sometimes the fire was lit and we would sprawl by the fire like bears. The fire would warm half a brother and then he would roll away and another brother would slide in and so on and so on. Sometimes the smaller brothers would fall asleep in the pile and our dad would eventually step in and with a mere glance part the waters and reach down like Zeus and elevate the child so gently that he never awoke until the next morning when he was startled to find himself in bed and not on the raft of his brothers.

Sometimes there *would* be wrestling and grappling and jockeying and edging and pinning and elbowing, and occasionally there would be fisticuffs, and Mom would grow grim about the mouth, but that is not what I want to remember this morning. I want to remember when we were scattered on the floor like stalks and husks, like sticks and poles, like skitter and duff. I want to remember the indolent sandy sneakery scent of my brothers heaped around me like piers and jetties and beams. It didn't happen that much. It needed an occasion. The cousins are visiting in flocks and gaggles. The neighbors are stopping by in sheaves and delegations. Jesus is just born and wrapped in rough cloth or just arisen and bound in the finest linen. It is a late summer afternoon and we have been at the beach all day and we are lazy and weary and salted with sand and we smell like sunlight and mustard and somewhere among us is a moist towel. One of us is telling a story and the others are half-listening and I am trying to listen but the story begins to ripple and fade, and soon we will shower, and then it will be dinner, and soon our sister will stalk through the wrack and drift of her brothers, looking silently for that wet towel, and she will snatch it suddenly like a heron snatches a minnow, the towel wriggling desperately as it is hauled to its doom, but that will not be for a while, and I have my legs flopped over one brother and my head propped against another, and somewhere in the pile a brother is telling a story about something green and liquid-fast, a fish or a car or a bird, and you would think that such seemingly slight moments as these would fade over the years, crowded and jostled as they are by facts and pain and love and loss; but your body remembers what your mind cannot. Your body forgets nothing.

God: a Note

Had a brief chat with God the other day. This was at the United States Post Office. God was manning the counter from one to five, as he does every blessed day. He actually says *every blessed day* and he means it. You never saw a more patient being. He never loses his cool and believe me he could. *I* would. I have been on line behind crazies at his window and heard vituperative abuse and vulgar character assassination and scurrilous insinuation and never once did I witness any flash of temper in response to this on his part. I have asked him how he could maintain his cool and he says things like *I try to put myself in their position* and *Witnessing catharsis is part of the job* and *All storms blow over* and *It's only frustration* and *There are so many much more serious things* and *We are all neighbors in the end.* I am impressed by these sentiments, in large part because I share them consistently only in theory and not always in practice. God, however, does not waver nor does he fluctuate in his equanimity. He stands there quietly as people bang their fists on his counter and offer rude remarks and stomp away muttering darkly. He does not smile when someone gets upset. He says he has learned that some people get more upset if you smile when they are upset. He listens to what they say and often, I notice, he makes a note on a pad as they leave. *I make a note if I think they have a good point we should discuss with management,* he says. Often what is couched as a complaint is actually a good point about how we could be of better service. He remembers pretty much every regular who comes to his window and he greets them politely by name. Sometimes he will inquire after children and animals. Dogs adore God and will sometimes rear up on his counter to see him better. He greets them politely by name surprisingly often. *I would guess I know a hundred dogs by name*, he says. *Hardly any cats. People don't take their cats with them when they go to the Post Office.* I make a joke about how cats are the children of Lucifer and he does not smile and I realize later that probably Lucifer is still a deeply sad and touchy subject for him. How would *you* feel if one of your best friends, one of your most trusted companions, tried to steal everything you had and were and did, and for this breathtaking betrayal he was cast shrieking into the darkness, no longer the Shining One, the Morning Star, but the very essence of squirming withered despair, until the end of time? Wouldn't you be haunted and sad about that ever after? I would. I felt bad and told God I was sorry about making a stupid joke. I said I made stupid jokes all the time even though I was now an older citizen and ought to have learned by now to not be so flippant. And God said, *No worries*, and *Better a poor joke than something worse*, and *Did I want to use the book rate for my package, which would save me about five bucks*, and I said yes, sir, and thank you, and I walked out of the Post Office thinking that if we cannot see God in the vessels into which the electricity of astonishing life is poured by a profligate creation, vessels like this wonderfully and eternally gracious gentleman at the Post Office, then we are very bad at the religion we claim to practice, which says forthrightly that God is everywhere available, if only we remove the beam from our eyes, and bow in humility and gratitude for the miraculous, which falleth even as the light from the sun, which touches all beings, and is withheld from none. So it is that I have seen God at the United States Post Office, and spoken to him, and been edified and elevated by his grace, which slakes all those who thirst; which is each of us, which is all of us.

The Kid Brother

Yes, we tossed him like a football when he was two years old. We did. And yes, we folded him like a smiling gangly awkward puppet into a kitchen cabinet. We did that. Yes, we painted his face blue once, and sent him roaring into our teenage sister's room to wake her up on a Saturday. We did that. Yes, we stood in the hospital parking lot with our dad and waved up at the room where our mom stood in the window brandishing our new kid brother who looked from where we stood like a bundle of laundry more than a kid brother. Yes, we gawped at him with disappointment when he came home and was placed proudly on the couch like a mewling prize and we muttered later quietly in our room that he seemed totally useless, brotherwise. We kept checking on him the rest of the day and he never did do anything interesting that we noticed, not even wail or bellow like babies did in the movies and on television, even when you poked him with a surreptitious finger. He just sprawled there looking perfect and after a while we lost interest and we went upstairs to plot against our sister.

As he grew he remained the most cheerful compliant complaisant child you ever saw, never complaining in the least when we tossed him or decked him or chose him last for football games or sent him in first as lonely assault force in conflicts of all sorts, and we were always half-forgetting him when we dashed off on adventures and expeditions, and we were always half-absorbed by and half-annoyed with his littlebrotherness,

11

happy to defend him adamantly against the taunts and shoves of others but not at all averse to burling him around like a puppy ourselves. We buried him in the sand up to his jaw at the beach. We spoke to him curtly and cuttingly when we felt that he was the apple of the grandmotherly eye and we were the peach pits, the shriveled potato skins, the sad brown pelts of dead pears. We did that.

And never once that I remember did he hit back, or assault us, or issue snide and sneering remarks, or rat on us to the authorities, or shriek with rage, or abandon us exasperated for the refuge of his friends. Never once that I can remember, and I am ferociously memorious, can I remember him sad or angry or bitter or furious. When I think of him I see his smile, and never any other look on his face, and isn't that amazing? Of how many of our friends and family can that be said? Not many, not many; nor can I say it of myself.

But I can say it of my kid brother, and this morning I suggest that those of us with kid brothers are immensely lucky in life, and those of us without kid brothers missed a great gentle gift unlike any other; for older brothers are stern and heroic and parental, lodestars to steer by or steer against, but kid brothers, at least in their opening chapters, are open books, eager and trusting, innocent and gentle; in some deep subtle way they are the best of you, the way you were, the way you hope some part of you will always be; in some odd way, at least for a while, they were the best of your family, too, the essence of what was good and true and holy about the blood that bound you each to each.

Often, I remember, we would be halfway down the street before one of us realized we had forgotten our kid brother, and we would grudgingly wrench our bicycles to skidding halts, and wait impatiently for him to catch up, under the nodding maples; and it says something deep and true and holy about my kid brother, who grew up to be a wonderfully generous and stalwart and patient and trustworthy man, that often now I find myself feeling somehow that he is slightly ahead of me, waiting with a smile, and I am pedaling furiously, trying to catch up with him.

Is That Your Real Nose?

B est questions I have been asked? As a writer? (This obviates all the wild questions I have been asked by my children, many of them cast in the most rude and vulgar terms imaginable, and the startling questions I have often been asked by my lovely bride, and even the questions the house wolf asks me with his ears, although those questions are generally straightforward ones like *can I eat this cat, or is that frowned upon socially?*)

The best ever: *Is that your real nose?* Asked of me by a moppet in kindergarten, where I was, no kidding, a visiting writer for a day, because the kids had *had my novel read to them over the course of a year!* Every day for half an hour in Story Time! Isn't that the most amazing and moving thing ever? I said yes, it was my real nose, why did she ask? And she said Because it's *really big*, and there's a bend or hump or something in it, and I explained that the Coherent Mercy had granted me many brothers in this wild and lovely life, which explained what happened to my nose.

Next best: *Why in all of your work is there no mention whatsoever of the radical lesbian community in Australia?* Asked of me by a woman in Australia, who was sitting in the front row and glaring at me with a ferocious and inarguable glare. For an instant I thought of making some snide comic retort, like well, there are no sun bears or hockey players in my work either, but then I snapped awake and felt a hint of her pain, and a shred, perhaps, of the bruised life she had lived, being sneered at by society because of the gender of the people she loved. Who cares about the gender of the people you love? Isn't loving and being loved the point? Isn't that what we talk about when we talk about religion and community? I didn't answer her question. I felt helpless and sad and there wasn't anything to say so I didn't say anything and then someone asked me about my hilarious headlong serpentine riverine sinuous sprinting prose style, and the conversation went in a different direction. I still think about that woman, though, and hope she found some sort of peace in her life. Rage burns you out.

Next best, asked of me recently by a high-school girl so far in the back of the dark auditorium that I could not see her but only heard her voice emerging from the dark like a sudden nighthawk: *How do you retain your dignity when you know and we know that most of the kids in this auditorium are not paying any attention to what you are saying at all?* This one I hit out of the park. This one I was ready for. This one I have been waiting to be asked for years. First of all, I said, I have three children, and they are teenagers, so I am very familiar and comfortable with not being listened to. Second, I was a teenager once, and believe me I was more sneery and rude and dismissive and snotty than any ten of you collectively, so I know how you feel. Third, and not to be rude, but I don't care if you have the guts to drop your masks and listen to what I have to say. You want to hide behind the wall of ostensible cool, be my guest. You want to live in the world of pretend where you perform some role all day rather than try to dig other people's joy and pain and courage, swell. Best of luck.

Not me. It took me the longest damned time to come out from behind my masks, it took me deep into my twenties, and if you want to be as stupid as me, swell. It's your life you are wasting. Too bad. Me, personally, I think you might find one or two tiny things to think about, listening to old bumbling shaggy me up on this stage. You might be moved a little, or at least giggle, or hear something you open up shyly later and ponder for yourself. Maybe not. I make no promises. I am just an aging idiot addicted to stories, because stories matter, my friend, and if you do not catch and share stories that matter, you will have nothing but lies and sales pitches in your life, and shame on you if that's the case. But it's your life. One thing I have learned as a dad and a husband is that no one listens to me, and they ought not to, either. You ought to listen to your own true self. I can maybe help you tiptoe a little closer to that self by sharing stories that matter, but if you are too cool to play today, swell. Me, personally, I can tell you that either you eventually take those masks off or they will damn well be kicked off by life, but I suspect that's a lesson you have to learn for yourself. Me, I suggest that the sooner you wake up and get it that there actually *is* a wild grace and defiant courage in people, and there actually *are* stories that save and change lives, and that there *is* a lot more going on here than we can ever find words for, and that love and attentiveness and creativity *are* real and wild and immanent, the cooler and wilder a life you will enjoy while you have such a priceless and inexplicable thing as a life, which goes by awfully fast, my friend. Believe me, I know. Does that answer your question at all?

Yes, sir, she said. Yes, sir, it surely does.

Your First Rosary

Your grandmother gave it to you for your First Communion. It came in a hinged box just like the one in which engagement rings crouch importantly. She handed it to you after the epic Mass at which you received Your First Communion. You were still dressed in your awkward uncomfortable first dark suit in which you looked like a tiny businessman or your rustling uncomfortable white dress in which you looked like a tiny debutante. Your new shoes were slowly grinding blisters the size of quarters into your heels. There was a reception in the sunny chilly back yard with savory foods you and your brothers and sisters only ever see at weddings and wakes. Some aunts and uncles gave you envelopes with cash. Two aunts gave you envelopes with holes cut in such a manner that you could see the faces of Abraham Lincoln on the five and Andrew Jackson on the twenty. Your uncle who was usually the most testy and snide handed you an envelope with a face you did not know peering out of it. Your older brother looks over your shoulder and says that is Ulysses Grant and you are now a rich man. You had never seen a fifty-dollar bill until that moment, and you have not seen one since, and there is a small shy part of you that wishes powerfully even now that you had saved that fifty-dollar bill.

You might have saved it in the pages of the Bible you received from your mother and father that day also. Your father selected it from the plethora of Bibles available in the bookshops of the city, and your mother had wrapped it carefully in shining white paper, and when you opened it you felt your father's right hand on your left shoulder, and saw your mother staring at you with the sidelong half-smile you had loved your entire life since you became aware of it as an infant and thought of it as what people meant when they used the word love.

The rosary was blue glass, or rose glass, or black plastic, or white bone, or a deep burnished russet glowing bronze oak or mahogany. It nestled in a bed of crushed translucent paper. The beads were strung on infinitesimal metal links or tightly beautifully braided string. The crucifix had a tiny lean gaunt sagging Christ with his head fallen onto his chest in utter weariness and despair. You always felt bad for him when you saw him like this but it was hard to discuss this with adults because if you said something like *the poor guy* they would launch into apologetics or hermeneutics or muddled theology or a speech about how his death was actually Glorious, and he was Resurrected, and Our Holy Mother the Church Says, and etcetera and etcetera in the endless murky religious blather of adults who are not listening to what you mean, and all you meant was that you felt bad for the poor guy, all battered and bereft and alone. Sometimes you dreamed of being a warrior hero in the ancient Irish mode who could go back in time and punch out the imperial soldiers with deft powerful sharp blows and break Jesus out of jail and the two of you would sprint into the hills and he would put his bony hand on your shoulder when you were safe and say *thanks brother* instead of sagging to death alone and haunted on a blunt cross on the Hill of Skulls.

You are supposed to put your new rosary back in the special celebratory box but there is something tactile and sinuous and riverine and finger-friendly about it, and you thumb the beads for a while quietly, and one aunt sees this and thinks you are praying and she spills her wine but we are out in the yard so it does not matter. Later she will tell your mother that she thinks you are chosen by the One to be a priest or a nun because she saw you fingering the rosary and your mother will try not to laugh although it's a close call.

One of your small cousins reaches for your new rosary but you know that it will break into a thousand glittering pieces if he touches it because he is the Destroyer, and his slightest touch can drain batteries and snap spectacles and deflate basketballs, so you slip the rosary into your jacket pocket, or your new white shining plastic purse, and fend off the Destroyer with the arrow of your elbow, and he goes off to break a bicycle or a door-jamb, and the uncles all have a second beer, because it's a special occasion and they are not driving and it's sunny, which is why God made beer, to be enjoyed on sunny days; Saint Augustine said so, you could look it up.

Much later, late at night, when you are in bed, and your brother or sister across the room is snoring like an asthmatic badger, same as usual, you suddenly remember your rosary, and you get up stealthily, and retrieve it from your pocket or purse, and tiptoe back to bed, pausing briefly to wonder if a gentle kick will stop that horrendous snoring, and you huddle under the blankets, and create your tight little cocoon in which warmth is trapped and you can hardly hear that awful snoring like someone sawing a table in half with a butter-knife, and you finger the rosary again for a while, with complicated feelings. You want to be cynical about the whole thing, because you are cool, but it's also a gift from your grandmother, who can be flinty but she means well under her glowering mask, and your dad had his hand on your shoulder, which is Dad Language for *I love you*, and your mom shone that sidelong half-smile at you like a bolt of light, and the rosary is a river in your hands, and you do feel bad for the poor guy, and ever since you were little there has been something alluring and mysterious and ancient about the rosary being chanted and mumbled and muttered and sung, on the radio and in church and in the house sometimes, when there is tension; the unutterably old music of call and response, the back and forth, the twin halves of the Hail Mary, the forthright honest litany of the Our Father; and you finger the beads, glass or bone or plastic or wood, and you whisper a few Hail Marys just to take the rosary out for a spin, as it were, and then somehow without meaning to you say a decade, and then another, and just as you are dimly trying to remember which Mysteries are Joyful and which are Glorious, and what conceivable difference could there be between them, you fall asleep.

Exactly one hour later, to the exact second that you slid into sleep, your father comes up to check on the kids, and he sees you with the rosary tangled in your fingers, and he silently goes downstairs and gets your mother, whose hands are soapy as she turns toward him questioningly from the sink, but she knows him, and she rinses her hands and dries them on that old blue towel, and she comes upstairs too, and they stand over your bed for a few minutes, in the moonlight. Neither of them says a word, but they never forget those few moments, and even now sometimes, for no reason at all, all these years later, one of them remembers, and says something quietly to the other, and they both smile and feel a pang of joy and glory and sorrow. As it was in the beginning is now, and ever shall be, world without end, amen.

Those Few Minutes

Here's another little thing that isn't. Not to me, anyway. Many years ago I played on a basketball team in Boston. Men's league, guys in their twenties, some of them very good ballplayers indeed. We had one of those guys. He had played college ball. Terrific athlete—he was, entertainingly, a world-class Frisbee player, whose ultimate Frisbee team had actually, no kidding, won the first world title, in Sweden. Great hoop player, though, smooth and graceful and efficient and generous, a wonderful passer.

Among the little quirks in his game, and there were many, including the occasional wearing of Mardi Gras beads on the court, was this one: when we formed our layup line to warm up before a game, he liked to slap the backboard after the ball left his hand. The first few times he did this we laughed; then slowly and wordlessly, in the way of such things, we all began to do it, because it was funny and silly and annoyed the other teams, who thought we were showing off or somehow deriding them. We did it in winter league, in tiny hot gyms, and we did it in summer league, outdoors under the towering elms and oaks of the parks where we played. Sometimes we riffed on it, with extra beats, and sometimes one guy would slap the backboard hard enough to make it shake, and so throw off the next guy's shot, and we would all snicker, and every other game or so the ref would mutter to our captain that if we did that in the game he would call a technical foul, and our captain would report this to us with high glee, and we would snicker again, and then the game would start.

Well, our guy with the beads got sick. He got major sick. He got a sick where your body slowly closes up shop and eventually you die when your heart and lungs close up shop. It was awful to watch. It's awful enough to watch in anyone but it's really awful when an unreal athlete gets that kind of sick and that graceful smooth vessel in which he expressed his joy grinds to a halt and collapses. He could shoot with either hand, the only player I ever saw who could actually do that, although many a player has tried. He loved hitting ridiculous shots, and then turning to us and laughing aloud that such an insane shot had dropped right through the middle of the hoop, rippling the net in such a way that occasionally the net would get caught on the rim and someone would have to jump up and pull it down again.

He died. Sure he did. No one comes back from the kind of sick he had—not yet, although a lot of his friends still do fundraisers all these years later, to try to help the medical world invent a way for people to make a comeback from that kind of sick. Not yet, though. Someday, maybe.

But here's the little thing I wanted to tell you. After he died a bunch of us were playing basketball one night, in one of the parks where we used to play summer league ball. There were eight of us and we stretched and taped our ankles and chaffed and asked about wives and girlfriends and jobs and first kids, and then we were going to split up and play four-on-four, but as we ambled onto the court to warm up this little thing happened: We got back into our old layup line, and the first guy, our subtle brilliant point guard, drove in for a layup, and slapped the backboard. The next guy slapped the board also and we all got the message and just for a few minutes that night eight guys drove for lazy layups and slapped the backboard, and then one guy slapped it so hard that the board shivered and the next guy's layup squibbed away, and we all snickered, and then the game started. But I wanted to tell you about those few minutes, when we did that little thing that wasn't little. I bet every one of us remembers those few minutes, too. There are many ways to pray.

A Tangle of Bearberry

My mother is driving me through the rain to the beach. I am applying for summer jobs. The rain is thorough and silvery. We do not speak. The trees along the road are scrubby and gnarled and assaulted by reeds. I am huddled in my jacket. No one else is on the road. You never thank your mother enough. The road is so wet that our tires send up tendrils and spouts of water behind us. I can see them flaring steadily in the mirror on my side. My mother is intent on the road. She would like to say something gentle about the interview I will have in a few minutes but she knows that I will not hear what she says. I will hear what I thought she said, which is not what she said. I heard a lot of what was not said or meant then instead of what was.

My mother woke me that morning, and fed me, and handed me clean folded clothes, and handed me the plethora of forms I was supposed to have filled out but had not filled out and of course filled out hurriedly scribbledly scrawlingly as she drove me through the rain to the beach. We drove along silently as I scribbled and she maybe thought about all the things she would have liked to say but was too wise to say.

This would have been a perfect time for me to say or whisper or even mumble my gratitude to my mother for eighteen years of extraordinary love and care. This would have been a great time for me to say something like I see your hard work, Mom, and I see your weariness with all these kids, and I see how quietly worried you and Dad are about money, and I can only faintly dimly imagine what it must be like to bear and coddle and raise and protect and educate and love children and have them be rude and vulgar and dismissive and contemptuous and worse. That would have been a great time for me to say something gentle for once. Rarely were we alone together for thirty minutes as we were that morning in the rain on the road to the beach. That would have been a great time for me to say quietly I see you, Mom, and I love you, and I never say that, and I should say that every thirty seconds every blessed day, and I should touch my head to the holy earth every dawn and say thank you for you to whatever it is that we mean when we say The Mercy and the Coherence and The Imagination. That would have been the perfect time, alone in the quiet car in the quiet rain on the silent road among the gnarled little trees.

By the time we got to the state park headquarters it was too late for me to say anything, and I hurried off to make the inter-view, and I don't know what my mother did for the next few minutes. Probably she went for a walk along the boardwalk, or sat in the car writing letters; she was always in motion, always quietly doing something even in moments when nothing needs to be done; that was how she was and still is, though now she moves very slowly indeed and does not drive at all. Now I drive, and she sits in the passenger seat, and we talk freely and cheerfully and deeply and avidly and eagerly and every time I talk to her I say I love you. We don't say that enough. We don't. After a while I came back from the interview and she started the car and we drove home through the ranks of the bent twisted little trees. There were pitch pines and salt cedars, and here and there beach plums, and thickets of sumac, and I thought I saw a tangle of bearberry but I could not be sure.

A Note on Martin Luther

I think we are in in agreement at this juncture that Martin Luther was absolutely correct and right *philosophically* when he nailed his Ninety-Five Theses on the Power and Efficacy of Indulgences to a chapel door in Wittenberg; the Catholic Church of his time was rife with greed and corruption and scandal and lies and theft and devious financial plots, as it still is, and probably always has been; such is the fate of entities run and staffed by human beings, from countries to corporations to city councils to colleges, although perhaps that will not always be their fate, if we ever manage to evolve away from snatching and hoarding, which is possible, if not probable.

But I maintain that Luther was utterly wrong and incorrect in his choice of *tools*. Why would you smash a *nail* into the lovely wooden door of All Saints Church? Could he not have used tape, or gum, or sap from the nearby towering and beloved village oak? Did he feel the slightest regret at punching a monstrous hole in a door that some poor workman had labored over for weeks? Imagine how *you* would feel if a Catholic monk (we forget that Luther was an Augustinian priest) showed up at your front door, the one you had specially made by your brother the master carpenter, who found some unbelievably beautiful black walnut, and planed it and carved it for months, and even installed it properly for you, because that is the kind of gracious and excellent guy he is, and then some portly *monk* storms up, and *hammers a nail* into your door? Would you feel all warm and grateful about this? You would not. You would shriek and rage, and stomp and storm, and roar and bluster, and set all three of the dogs on the guy, and chortle evilly as he sprinted away down the street, the dogs shredding his cassock, and then you would think seriously for a moment of stuffing some birch gum into that hole, and carefully painting over the hole with shoe polish or peanut butter, to match the russet color of the door, but then you would realize that your wife will eventually notice that, and sigh that sigh she sighs when you misuse the peanut butter, so you man up about the whole thing, and call your brother, and then you call the local religious authority, and file a blistering complaint for damages, and enclose a *very* nasty note to the priest's personnel file.

Again let me say that the paper that Luther nailed to the door was a very fine paper indeed; again and again the man makes the most perfect and admirable sense, and calls the Church he loved, and indeed had joined in a professional capacity, to task for vast and stunning lies and corruption; no reasonable soul could argue with his general propositions that the pope is not actually God, and ought not to be acquisitive financially, and money donated on earth does not actually expurgate the sins of those who have died. Nor can any reasonable soul argue with the tidal shift that Luther's tart note then caused in the long history of Christianity; while we may rue the splits and calvings, we must admire the impulse toward honesty and piety that drove those shearings away, even as we daydream about some sort of Great Détente, in which the myriad Christian traditions come back together under one flag or another, even, perhaps, as a tremendous tribe of defense and reverence for the faith Christ himself practiced, which is to say eternally besieged Judaism.

No, no—we can have nothing but great respect and even a sort of awe for Martin Luther the *author*—a brave man, taking on the fabulously wealthy powers of his day. But we ought to be aghast and appalled at the man with a terrible nail in his hand. He might have borrowed some glutinous material from a snail; he might easily have tapped an evergreen for a drop of its lifeblood; he might have snatched a cinnamon bun from a child, and used a dab of that awful gleaming sticky muck to affix the Theses. But no: a whopping nail, and a whole day's work for some poor guy who probably was all set to slip up into the mountains for a day to hunt ibex. In a just and fair world, Luther himself should have had to go back the next day and fix that hole, and not with peanut butter, either. Perhaps he did; he was, by all accounts, a decent sort, and it may well be that an hour after he posted his revolutionary document, he slapped himself on the forehead and went back to plug the hole. Let us hope so; in fact, let us pray that this was the way it was, on a cold November day, many years ago.

Our Daily Murder

Bless me, Father, for I have sinned, and I am totally wrestling with feeling bad about sinning, which I do a little and then don't at all—I'll explain. Yesterday a guy walked into a classroom in my state and shot nine people to death and shot up ten others so bad that they'll limp and be in pain in a dozen ways every hour the rest of their lives. A cop shot the shooter and now the shooter is dead. But this all happened too in Columbine and Aurora and Sandy Hook and Charleston and Norway and Dunblane and Tasmania and on and on and need I go on? And what is my sin? I'll tell you, Father. Lean in a little here so no one hears. I wanted to shoot the shooters. In the head. I did. And then when I calmed down I wanted to punch the idiots who immediately started shouting that this doesn't have anything to do with gun control. And then I wanted to thump the people who excoriated the school for not having armed guards on duty every fifty feet around the perimeter. And then I wanted to afflict everyone issuing comment and opinion and advice and soundbites with laryngitis that would last a month. And then all I could see were body bags and people sobbing. The mother and the father of the shooter sobbing and speechless. And I was ashamed of myself, Father, because *I* wriggle with violent impulses, and *I* have punched and thumped and shouted, and in me is the same squirm of lashing violence as in every other man and probably most women, if they were honest. So I come to you, Father, to see if you can help me. I need you to tell me this will end someday. I need you to tell me Christ was right and turning the other cheek will not always mean getting a knife slash on the other cheek too. I need you to tell me that this has nothing to do with easy useless labels like Satan and Evil and Insanity and everything to do with the brooding shadow in every heart. I need you to tell me that shadow will be dispersed and disseminated someday and not by fiat from the One but by us working our asses off to make violence something that you visit in the war museum. I need you to confirm that it's *us* who can solve our daily murder. I need you to confirm that Christ is in us and we can do this if we stop posturing and preening and labeling and actually do something about lonely idiots with brains full of worms. And we are not just talking about addled lonely boys with squirming brains, are we? Aren't we also talking about arrogant pompous blowhards like bin Laden and Hitler who are sure they know what's best and right for everyone? Aren't we talking about slimy wannabe caliphs who want to own a desert where they pretend it's the seventh century? Aren't we talking about everyone who thinks they knew best? Aren't we talking about that jagged splinter of bloody bile in every man's heart, and probably most women, if they were honest? Aren't we talking about your heart and mine, Father? What's *my* sin, really? Deeper than the rage I feel with people who murder innocents, people who close up their brains as they open their mouths? My sin, down deep, is that I often despair of us, Father. I do. At night. I don't wake my wife. She has enough to deal with. But I lie awake and think maybe we are exactly the same savage primates we were a million years ago, and culture and civilization are mere veneer, and we will always be pulling triggers in so many ways—pistols, rifles, cannons, drones, bombers, warheads, whatever brilliant murder tool we come up with next. We're so creative, eh, Father? Always looking for a new way to blow the other guy to bits and then drape righteous excuse over the bloody dirt. So that's what I wanted to tell you, Father. I rage, I despair. I am ashamed of that. Both are small. I want to be big. I want us all to be big. I want Christ to be right. I want the word *shooter* to be forgotten. I want us to outwit violence. But I am so often so afraid that we will always be small and Christ was a visionary whose words will drown in a tsunami of blood. I know *you* can't forgive me, Father. I know the drill. But I ask that you join me in intercession to the One for hope, for endurance, for a flash of his love like water when we are so desperately thirsty we think we will never find water again. Amen.

The Viewing

Walked into the chapel at dusk last night, and there she was, in the casket off to the left, with her son standing sentinel. He is a priest and he was smiling a little in welcome as people walked up to him and hugged him, if they were young, or shook his hand, if they were older men. The older men who shook his hand would take his right hand with their right hands and then cover the two clasped hands with their left hands, I noticed. A sort of a paternal or protective gesture which moved me very much for some reason.

The casket was half open and she was wearing a lovely demure dress but you couldn't see if she had her best shoes on. I assume she had her best shoes on. A pink glass rosary was wrapped around her hands. It being Wednesday I assume she would be praying the Glorious Mysteries, during which we meditate particularly on resurrection, ascension, and assumption. She knew what Mysteries we meditated upon every day of the week. She had prayed the rosary every day since she was three years old, I believe. Even when she was very ill she prayed the rosary every day and even when she could no longer remember her son's face or name she would still run her fingers over her rosary. I believe you can pray the rosary even if you no longer know what the word rosary means. Perhaps that is when the rosary is prayed most piercingly of all.

Her hair was done beautifully in the bouffant style which long ago went out of style but most assuredly never went out of style for her. If there is a photograph of her in this world without her hair carefully elevated and frozen magically in place by mysterious elixirs, I have not seen it, and I cannot believe it exists. She is wearing her scapula, which I believe she wore every day of her life since she was a child, and she is wearing a Marian medal, because she and the Madonna were very close friends, and talked to each other continually, especially when she lost her husband and their other son.

Her surviving son is now moving toward the sacristy, for he will preside tonight over the vigil service for his mother, but it takes him a while to make his way to the sacristy to robe up, because people keep hugging him or shaking his hand. *I will gather you with care*, the chapel choir is singing. I stand by the casket for a while. *I will hold you close to my heart*, sings the choir. A child of about nine peers over the edge of the casket fearfully. *We will run and not grow weary.* I feel for the child, because it *is* unnerving to see a dead person supine in the chapel, and she sure looks like she is frozen solid, which may come from faint dusting of powder on her face and hands. *We will rise again.* Her son the priest emerges from the sacristy and lines up with his altar servers. *Lift up your eyes and see who made the stars.* The congregation stands, rustling, and turns to watch the priest, their friend and companion, begin the service. He and his mother will go home to their native city tomorrow, by train, and there will be a rosary at night in their old parish, with their old neighbors and friends chanting back and forth in the dim candlelight, and a funeral Mass the next morning, and then she will be buried with her beloved husband and their other son. Her son the priest will not be buried with his brother and parents, but will someday sleep with his brother priests in a field with a low stone wall, along which students walk back and forth to class. I have seen the field and the stone wall and I have seen students run their hands gently along the wall as they walk past the hundreds of sleeping priests. *I know you, I call you each by name*. I pray with all my heart that this is so, and bless myself with water from the baptistry, and slip out of the chapel to be with my wife and children while yet we live; while yet we live.

The Game

A friend of mine is explaining, at herculean length, his happy addiction to fantasy football, and inasmuch as there is plenty of good wine, and several other ostensibly attentive listeners, my attention drifts a little, and sudden I am twelve years old, and it is midnight, and I am in my room in the back of the house, and everyone else is asleep, and I am sitting at my desk under the weak watery light of the ancient lamp, playing a dice baseball game.

The game is played with two dice and a pencil and a ruler and a notebook. I invented it. I do not remember how or why I would have done such a thing, as I was not and am still not a baseball fanatic. But I did invent it and I played it once or twice a day for years, mostly at night when everyone was asleep, but sometimes all the dim afternoon on wet dark cold days. You carefully mark out nine innings with the ruler, and then write out your opposing lineups, and check the back of the notebook for whose turn it is to pitch, and you have a sip of tea, and the game begins. You have to roll the dice actually on the notebook, so that they do not rattle against the battered old wooden desk, which would wake up a brother or two, but there are firm stern rules against deliberately rolling them into the notebook gutter to try to influence the outcome, and you abide by the rules, because you, as commissioner of the league, made the rules, and it would be bad form for you to flout the very rules you imposed on yourself; an early and halting lesson for me in moral conduct.

I do not remember the rest of the details of the game, what constituted strikes and balls and triples and hit-batsmen and steals and homers and wild pitches and walks and the other lovely intricate arcana of baseball. I do remember that I murmured a steady running account of the game, making up details as we went along, so that when for example the bases were loaded, and there were two outs, and the lefty batter stretched the count full, and everyone in the park leaned in excitedly for the pitch, and the dice inarguably declared that he was out, he was not merely and flatly out, but had anticipated the pitch perfectly, and read the spin from the pitcher's hand instantly with his astounding eyesight, and stepped into it with all his might, and got every bit of it with the sweet spot of his mammoth bat, and hammered a screaming line drive, which looked to everyone in the park, not to mention both dugouts and all the umpires, to be a laser shot to center, scoring one run and possibly two, or even *three* if the center fielder screwed it up, and the pitcher, a righty still in his follow-through toward the plate, makes an incredible twisting whirl to try to snag the ball as it rockets over his other shoulder, but he just misses, and everyone leaps up, but the brilliant second baseman, who was leaning to his right on the pitch because he saw the sign for curve and saw the catcher set up for a pitch tailing away from the batter, dives full out and makes an incomprehensible catch, you wouldn't *believe* a guy could make a play like that unless you saw it with your own naked eyeballs, and it was one of those amazing ice-cream-cone catches too where he just got enough of the ball to haul it in, and there was an inch of the ball sticking out of his battered old black glove as he held it up triumphantly to show the umpire, who makes the call with a look on his face something like awe that he was there to see this historic catch, and the park goes nuts, and the second baseman trots to the dugout grinning a little, and his teammates deliberately ignore him for a minute, just to razz him, and then everyone pounds him on the back and tousles his hair and exchanges complicated ritual handshakes, and we go to a commercial for Schlitz beer.

Sometimes I think this is how I started to be a writer.

Bunt

Freshman baseball practice, fourth or fifth day maybe, the last day before the final cuts and the team is set for the season, and for some reason the coach dictates bunting practice, and we all troop to the plate, one after another, for bunting practice, because bunting is *important*, and every man should know how to drop bunts in front of the plate, and execute drag bunts, and bunt toward third base or first base as required, and we should also learn how to chop-bunt, by slashing down at the pitch and deliberately hammering it into the patient dust, so that ideally it hops up so sharply that the onrushing pitcher watches helplessly as it hops over his head, are you paying attention here, boys?

Even the guys who clearly were going to make the team, and clearly would never be asked to bunt in their entire high-school careers, had to take bunting practice, and there was a good deal of razzing and ragging going on, because bunting is one of those dark baseball arts that not every good hitter is good at, like hitting sacrifice flies, and weirdly it seems like the worse the hitter the better the bunter, so that the scrawny infielders who could barely hit their weight were the best bunters, and the superb muscular athletes who consistently cracked doubles and occasionally homers were lesser bunters, for reasons that are murky. Why the smaller skinnier guys were better at manipulating the bat in this one particular specific arcane act is a mystery, but that appeared to be the case, which explained a great deal of the razzing and ragging.

The order in which guys went to the plate for bunting practice was pretty much the measure of how good they were at baseball and how likely they were to make the team, so I was near the end of the line, with only a couple of guys behind me at the tail end. I did predictably poorly, when it came to bunting, because I was afraid of the ball, a mean savage nasty stony pebble I could barely see and which hurt terribly when it hit you. I had been hit several times already, by pitches and ground balls and once, mortifyingly, by a fly ball, so I was leery, which did not help my bunting, which would have been awful anyway. I survived, though, and then my turn was over, and Fred came to the plate.

Fred was a geek. Fred was gawky and uncoordinated and had a silly haircut. Fred did not even have cleats and wore his sneakers and once he had slipped and fallen so comically in the outfield that even the coach lost it laughing. Fred was not going to make the team. He knew he was not going to make the team. Everyone knew. It wasn't that guys picked on him; it was that no one bothered to acknowledge him. I was no better than anyone else in this. I ignored him too. I have a vague memory of him extending his hand to say hello and me ignoring him and I believe that memory is vague because I am ashamed of it.

But, o inexplicable, o unimaginable, o incomprehensible, Fred could bunt. Each guy got ten pitches, and Fred stood there calmly, hands correctly aligned on the bat, feet squared up to the pitcher, and he dropped one lovely bunt after another: dribbled slowly up the third-base and first-base lines, twice each; twice chopped so hard it bounced six feet over the onrushing pitcher's head; twice dropped stone-cold-dead a few feet in front of the plate, exactly where no one would be able to get to it in time; once hit with such deft backspin that the ball leapt back toward the plate away from the startled shortstop's hungry hand; and finally a drag bunt executed so perfectly that one of the fathers in the stands, who did not realize that Fred was a geek, exclaimed in pleasure.

All this would be amazing enough, but it's the three or four seconds after this that I wanted to share with you. No one said a word. I don't think anyone even moved a muscle, other than Fred, who crossed first base and turned into foul territory to come back to the dugout. Just that—the absolute stillness, as Fred steps on the bag and turns toward the dugout. Just those few seconds, when no one said a word or even moved a muscle. Just that.

Eight Whopping Lies

This won't hurt a bit. Yes, it will. It will hurt so bad you will blubber like a Cubs fan. It will feel like someone shot an arrow into your tooth and the arrow went through your nether parts and is now sticking out of your knee. Any dentist or hygienist who actually says this should have to spend a day in a closet with the Reverend Al Sharpton as penance.

It is a peacekeeping operation. No, it isn't. It is an operation during which tall children will be shot in the face and shot in the groin and have their legs and faces blown off, and all because neither side of the argument had the wit to figure out another way to solve the problem other than choosing some of their brightest and most muscular children and paying them to die. Did you think human sacrifice had faded from the world? Not so. Not so at all.

God is on our side. No, he isn't, or she isn't, and how incredibly foolish to even assign human gender to something we all admit is so unimaginably epic that any shred of claim to knowledge, let alone possession or intimacy, is lunatic, not to mention murderous. "God, help us to tear their soldiers to bloody shreds with our shells," says Mark Twain, "help us to cover their smiling fields with the pale forms of their patriot dead; help us to drown the thunder of the guns with the shrieks of their wounded, writhing in pain; help us to lay waste their humble homes with a hurricane of fire; help us to wring the hearts of their unoffending widows with unavailing grief; help us to turn them out roofless with little children to wander unfriended the wastes of their desolated land in rags and hunger and thirst..."

It's not you, it's me. No, it's pretty much you she didn't fall in love with, or fell out of love with, or fell in love with someone else instead of. This doesn't mean you are a flawed and scurrilous being, not at all. It *does* mean it's you whom he or she does not love, or no longer loves, though. Let's at least get that straight.

A baby inside a mother is not a person. Sure, she is. Alive is alive, and dickering over what counts as a person is blather designed to let us tiptoe away from the fact that someone died. But people die all the time for all sorts of reasons. We kill prisoners in jail, we kill other countries' soldiers and civilians, we sell gobs of alluring products that lead to death, a lot of babies die after they are born, from being abandoned and starved and beaten. We are pretty comfortable with people dying, isn't that so? So why bother to pretend the dead person was not a person?

It's not about the oil. Sure it is. If there was an incredibly cruel dictator squirming in a land without vast reserves of oil, and he (dictators are always male, why is that?) made loud donkey noises about weapons, would we start a long savage war there? No? Are we at war with the dictator in North Korea who is the third in his family to starve his own people? No? Did we go to war with Charles Taylor, Robert Mugabe? No? Any pattern here?

We are stewards of America's land and water, and we do our utmost to protect our national legacy, and similarly beautifully phrased and designed full-page ads from Exxon and BP and mining companies. But those are whopping epic egregious astounding lies. Actually you are *terrible* stewards, and you grudgingly do only the minimum as required by law, if that, and you would happily dodge that if you could, so as to elevate share price. You know that, and we know that, and if you really *were* stewards you would go into another business altogether. You assume, reasonably, that you can dodge most legal action, or outspend the shrill screaming greens, and dump the company the instant you decide you have maxed out the profit margin. We all know this. It's excellent business. We won't pass harsher laws, because that would trammel the market, so you're good to go. Thanks for the lovely advertisements, though. They may be the last place to see clean water, in the end.

My campaign is all about family values. No, it isn't. If that was the case, why are there fifteen million American children who don't have enough to eat today? Why are there eight million kids with no health care? Why do so many kids have one parent, and no place to live, and never go to school, and get raped and beaten every blessed day? If your campaign was really about family values, would you ever rest until there were no kids weeping in dark corners in your city and state and country? Well? Wouldn't you?

Pull-up Pants

By chance last night I found myself shuffling down the grocery aisle lined with diapers and sippy-cups and breast-pumps and assorted other baby paraphernalia, all of which I half-noticed until I came to the shelves on which resided ever so many brightly colored pull-up pants, and there I paused and pitched camp for several long moments, and gazed happily upon the myriad offerings with pleasure and amusement and genuine nostalgia, so much so that another dad walking by laughed, because we knew without speaking that we were cousins in the clan of men who have wrestled pull-up pants on and off their small children, and specified in no uncertain terms that you may *not* wear your pull-up pants on your head, and you may *not* both wear pull-up pants on your heads like rustling helmets and have a jousting match with brooms, and you may *not* sell your Bert pull-up pants to your brother for a quarter because he wants the Bert pants and not the Ernie pants and it was *his* turn for the Ernie pants and Dad is *icky* and life is *icky* and he is appealing to a higher court who says with her usual blunt maternal grace that if he does not climb into those Bert pants in three seconds or less he will be sentenced to the *Elmo* pants, and no man in his right mind wishes to be seen in Elmo pull-up pants.

Many is the time, brothers and sisters, many is the time I stalked this very aisle looking for pull-up pants with certain beloved faces on them and *not* certain other faces, and staggered back to the checkout girl with not one but two massive bales of pull-up pants as vast as the bales of cotton once carried by groaning mules in the steaming fields of Mississippi, and paid handsomely for the privilege of bringing the bales home and having children use them fast and furious for all sorts of purposes, including sometimes the one for which they were designed; but also the pull-up pants were braided into an incredible rope to save one boy who was lost in the sea of the rug while the other one was steering the boat of his bed, and once the pull-up pants were wrestled heroically onto the leg of the dog before they (the pull-up pants) were shredded beyond recognition into so many tiny scraps that the vacuum cleaner gagged and died; and pull-up pants adorned basketballs and footballs and soccer balls, and they were the subject of many piercing questions about Dad's childhood, such as did people even *have* pull-up pants that long ago, before fire was invented?

I stood there in the diaper aisle, sisters and brothers, and I laughed aloud at the memories, and I wondered, for the thousandth time, at the weirdness and wonder of our culture, that we put the cheerful faces of puppets on pull-up pants, I mean, whose great idea was that? And I felt a great sadness also, that my children are long past pull-up pants, and never again will I be seriously weighing shrill appeals for the *Ernie* pants, or debating the relative merits of Buzz Lightyear pants v. Woody pants, the Woody pants are *not* loser pants, Woody is a cool guy and he is the sheriff and he has an excellent *hat*, and yes, I *know* Buzz can fly, or thinks he can, and yes, the pants with a guy who can fly are arguably cooler than the pants with a guy who *cannot* fly, you have an excellent point, but you had the Buzz pants yesterday, so my unappealable ruling is that *you* wear Woody and your brother gets Buzz today, and do not use the word icky with *me*, young man. As for your other questions, yes, you can eat peanut butter out of the jar with a spoon, and no, you cannot shave the dog, and no, I did not wear pull-up pants because they were not invented when I was a boy, we used diapers made of cedar fibers and deerskins that my grandmother had chewed to a remarkable supple softness. Did Grandfather wear pull-up pants? That is an *excellent* question. Let's call him and ask and I bet he will make that sound like he is swallowing an otter, isn't that the coolest sound ever?

Death of a Grocery Store

One of the three old grocery stores in our town is closing slowly. Its demise was announced a month ago, a casualty of corporate chess, and week by week the discounts mount and the shelves grow thin. The fish counter is empty and dark and the tall dour man who ran it transferred to another store two towns west. The meat counter is empty and dark and the sweet-faced cheerful girl who ran it took the buyout and is going to take one more stab at college. All the good wines in the wine section are gone and the only wines remaining are the ones you might use for cooking if you were desperate. The checkout men and women are artificially cheerful and when you mention how sad and bedraggled the store looks they smile and say *it's almost baseball season!*, and you realize they are weary weary weary of talking about the demise of the store and how it was a central gathering point for every single person for a mile around and how because it stayed open until midnight you could swing by for milk or diapers or cough medicine so late at night that no one else was on the road except cops and the patrons of taverns.

The discount bread bin where you could buy day-old bread and pies for half-price is empty. The vast epic incredible alluring array of cheeses from which occasionally my sons were allowed to pluck one sight unseen no longer stretches all the way from canned foods to fresh produce. The fresh produce is now only hardier stuff like apples and oranges and potatoes and turnips.

The only cookies remaining are the ones with that horrifying fake plastic frosting that no sane person would eat if you want to retain any of your teeth. The movie-rental box the size of a whopping refrigerator is gone, recalled by its lord and master. The iron bin from which the kids loaded firewood into the trunk of the car is empty. The recycling shed is forlorn. The plastic buckets from which flowers once called plaintively to you as you shuffled past are empty. The shelves of pills and salves and ointments and treatments and elixirs are stripped of toothpastes and lotions and the more colorful vitamins. The frozen food aisle still seems full; but when I look closely all that remains are the expensive items, like shrimp cakes made of shrimp with college educations, and all the humble frozen vegetables are gone.

It wasn't the cleanest store, and more than once I saw wilted things, and things slightly past their expiration date, and spills on aisle nine that took so long to be cleaned up that you could see the shadow of the spill for weeks afterwards. The recycling shed always reeked of beer and cigarettes, the parking lot gleamed with oil slicks, and the newspapers for sale were almost always from the day before, which is to say a century ago, by our modern measure.

Yet the store was steady and sturdy, and its denizens were my neighbors, and its staffers were efficient and workmanlike and friendly under any and all conditions. The store refused to close during snowstorms. The store welcomed huddled gasping refugees from terrific windstorms. The store happily sponsored baseball and soccer teams, and donated canned food to the local food bank, and allowed Girl Scouts to pitch their annual cookie camps by the door. The store employed many of my neighbors and fed the rest. The cashiers knew a thousand residents by name and gently bent the rules for a few who needed help; many times I saw a neighbor of mine who wanders the streets all day come into the store, and shuffle to the coffee corner, and pour himself a cup, and shuffle right back out without paying, and no one said a word, no one berated or barked at or reported him, because they knew him to be poor and gentle and addled, and who would begrudge that man a cup of coffee here and there, against the lonely shuffle of his days and years?

The store closes for good next week, and the building will sit empty for a while, and then a new tenant will come, floating balloons and issuing free coupons; or the building will be dismantled carefully by expert bulldozers, and another structure will arise; but I suspect that for many years to come my neighbors and I will say *where the store used to be* when we refer to that space in this wild green world; and after we say those words there will come a brief vision of the store when it was healthy and alive, bustling and busy, with avocados two for one today, and fresh snapper on sale, and yes, we can buy a watermelon if you boys can carry it out, and yes, I paid for the firewood, thanks for loading that in, boys, and yes, both of you can choose one cheese each from the wall today, close your eyes first, hold my hand, ready?

The Four Gospels

The first time I ever entered the tiny subterranean apartment of the woman who would eventually marry me, I was struck by a number of things: her large and not especially friendly dog, who regarded me with understandable suspicion; the lack of any extraneous furniture or appurtenances other than those required by an artist who was also a superb cook; and her one small rickety bookshelf, perched over her bed, so that she could reach up with one hand, while supine, and haul down an inky companion, therein to ramble and plumb.

Being a writer, I went right to the bookshelf, which was also blessedly away from the grim and gimlet-eyed dog, and examined her collection. There were four books and four books only, although I later discovered she was a ferocious and omnivorous reader; she later explained that her days were so crammed with work and school that if she had a few moments to read at night she counted herself lucky, and these four books were, perhaps, talismans of a sort, touchstones, compass points, lodestars, old friends, necessary and nutritious companions.

I remember them well, I remember how they leaned on each other there on the incredibly rickety shelf (the whole apartment was like that, and I felt like an unruly giant whose slightest misstep or sneeze would bring tables and shelves crashing to the floor), and I report with a smile that she still owns all four of the books, though now they are surrounded by many other books, for we have been married for nearly thirty years, and our collections long ago merged and mixed and mingled, and now Ellen Gilchrist rubs up against Bernard DeVoto, and Peter Matthiessen shoulders Laurie Colwin, and Annie Dillard is cheek by jowl with Alberto Giacometti, and other interesting pairings like that, you wonder what riveting conversations are had on the shelves at night when all is otherwise still, until Joseph Conrad whispers to Elinor Lipman…

There was Willa Cather's fine *Song of the Lark*, and Harper Lee's perfect *To Kill a Mockingbird*, and David James Duncan's great headlong Pacific Northwest coming-of-age novel *The River Why*, and best of all, greatest of all, the glorious hilarious epic sprawling wondrous novel *The Horse's Mouth*, by the Irishman Joyce Cary, and that was all, just those four, the three lean and the one thick with Cary's word-wizardry; and now I look back through the years at that shelf and wonder if those four books did not nearly encapsulate and characterize and explain and draw a collective map to the woman who married me.

There was a Northwest classic, filled with burling rivers and dense spruce forests and laughter and love and confusion and epiphany and rain; and those are her things, her place, her scent. There was the story of an American woman rising to be a terrific artist, and realizing that she could steer her own life, and not be beholden to a lover or a husband or the harness, however pleasant, of family; and this is her lifelong work and story. There is the story of a bright brave American girl and a beloved stalwart father, who teaches integrity and grace by his very being; and that is her story, and her father. And there is the novel I love above all others, filled with humor and struggle and prickly grace and a yearning to marshal color and shape and paint and canvas in such ways as to sing and celebrate the entire universe and everything in it; and that is her life and work and story, as I have had many occasions to see.

I am sure she did not choose those four books as a message to such amorous suitors as me; I am sure she did not herself consider that they might collectively say something piercing and eloquent about she who owned them, and gathered them together like a musical quartet on that most rickety of shelves; but it seems to me now that amazingly they did and do speak clearly and penetratingly of she who carried them from one ocean to another, many years ago, and occasionally reached up behind her head with one hand, when she was supine and weary, and hauled down a friend, who spoke to her of character and courage, grace and humor, love and imagination, rain and affection, and so much more. Those are very good books on their own merits, but to me, and I believe to my lovely bride, they will always be great books for other reasons, some of them too subtle for words.

The Old Typewriter in the Basement

Once again a student asks me how I became a writer, and this time I say, Because of the staccato staggered music of my dad's old typewriter in the basement. Because when he really got it going you could listen to it like a song. Because after a while you could tell if he was writing a book review or a letter just from the shift and drift of the thrum of the thing. Because it sounded cheerful and businesslike and efficient and workmanlike and true. Because a bell rang when he came to the end of a line, and you could hear him roll sheets of paper in and out of the carriage, and you could imagine him carefully lining up the carbon sheet to the face sheet, and he typed with two fingers faster than anyone we knew could type with ten, and he had the professional journalist's firm confident knowledgeable hammer-stroke with those forefingers, as if his blunt sinewy forefingers knew perfectly well what they wanted to say and were going about their business with a calm alacrity that you could listen to all day long.

Because his typewriter had dozens of deft machined metal parts and they had cool names like spool and platen and ribbon. Because his typewriter was a tall old typewriter that he loved and kept using even when electric typewriters hove into view and tried to vibrate onto his desk. Because if you stared closely at the keys, as I did quite often, you could see which letters he used more than other letters. Because the typewriter *was* him and he was our hero and we loved him and we wanted to be like him which is why we all learned to type. Because you would daydream of writing a story on his typewriter but you would never actually *do* so because using his typewriter would be like driving God's car which you would hesitate to do for fear you would break something and feel bad about that until Judgment Day when all is forgiven even stripping the gears on God's Ford Taurus.

Because his typewriter stood proudly in the center of his desk and there were books and magazines and dictionaries and neat stacks of paper and manila folders and newspaper clippings and rulers and erasers and pencils and pens and a jar of rubber cement and not one but two X-acto knives sharper than a falcon's talons on his desk also, and above his desk was a shelf crowded with dictionaries and catechisms and manuals and other books of all sorts, many of them bristling with bookmarks and scraps of paper marking particular pages or passages of heft and verve and dash and wit.

Because when he went downstairs to his desk you could be in any room upstairs even unto the attic and hear the first hesitant strokes as he began typing, and then the sprint and rattle and rollick as he hit his stride, and when he really had it going you would hear an impossibly short pause between the end of one page and the start of another, a break so brief that you could not *believe* he could whip one sheet out and whirl another in so fast unless you saw it with your own eyes which we did sometimes peeking from the door of the study into which no child was allowed when Dad was typing for fear you would interrupt his thoughts which were no kidding Putting Food on the Table, you will not under any circumstances interrupt your father when he is in his study, if you are bleeding come upstairs and bleed, and inform me of the cause of bleeding, and if you cannot find me find your sister, and if you cannot find either of us stanch the bleeding with a hand-towel, *not* a bath-towel, and go next door and ask the neighbors for assistance if necessary. Soak the towel in cold water afterward.

Because he had been typing since he was a boy, and because all the love letters he wrote to our mother when he was far away deep in the tropics in the war were meticulously typed, and the poems he sent were meticulously typed, and because he told me once that he had several times in his thirties tried to rise before dawn to type a novel, even as the house was filled with small children and he was due on the early train to his press job in the city, but he did not have the energy to invent and embroider, and he would fall asleep with his head in his arms on the typewriter, and startle awake after a while, and never finish his novels.

But I have written novels, and there are times, many times, when I think that I have done so in large part because of him, and his old typewriter, and the sound of his cheerful efficient staccato typing in the basement. Because he is still our hero and we love him and we want to be like him more than ever. Because maybe my novels are somehow the novels he started to write and could not finish. Perhaps somehow I have finished them for him and he startles awake and grins ruefully at his old typewriter and pads upstairs to wake the kids and I am typing these last words with my forefingers and with tears sliding slowly into my beard.

Have Ye Here Any Meat?

The Christos, for a skinny guy, sure was interested in good things to eat: he is constantly talking about bread and wine and oil and grain and seeds and vineyards, and he turns a hundred-some gallons of water into excellent wine, and he turns two fish (probably sardines) and five loaves of barley bread into so much food that twelve basketsful of bread shards remain after five thousand people have eaten, and he grills fish (probably St. Peter's fish, or tilapia) and bread on the shore of the Sea of Galilee; and even after he died and traveled unto the nether reaches of hell, and was returned by the word of the Father to life, and walked along the road to Emmaus expounding learnedly, and appeared suddenly amid the rattled remaining eleven disciples in a locked room, he is still absorbed with food, for the first question he asks his followers is this: Have ye here any meat?

And they gave him a piece of broiled fish, and of a honeycomb, and he took it, and did eat before them, which you can totally understand, as he must have been waspish with hunger after three days without food. And while troops of scholars have opined that his eating fish and honey is an editorial signifier of his actual corporeal resurrection, and we are to understand his breaking of bread and sharing of water and wine as the first Eucharist, I would like to not so politely insist that there is a blunt salty side to these gustatory reports that we do ill to forget or ignore; for they are there, scattered amid all the

Gospels, not for symbolic reasons, I think, but because they *happened*, and he actually *said* those things, and he was a guy, a dude, a bro, a youngish man, in fact, just past thirty, with dusty feet and a peevish temper sometimes (remember his tantrum in the temple), and a snippy tone sometimes (he actually says 'woman, what have I to do with thee?' to his mother at Cana, can you imagine saying that in that tone to *your* mother?), and hungry most of the time, fond of the breaking of bread.

If he is only a story, a legend, a fable, a faint and faraway hero, a target to whom we direct our muddled prayers, he is nothing. If he is only a hero, a superstar, a superior order of being, he is nothing. The inexplicable genius of Christianity is that it is nonsensical and unreasonable and impossible: a gaunt Arab Jew, speaking Aramaic and Hebrew, copper-skinned, short, slight of build, skilled only in carpentry and scholarly analysis of the Torah, often testy and gnomic when he spoke— *this* unknown obscure unassuming fellow was the incarnation of That which dreamed and spoke everything that is into being? The star child, the chosen one, the distilled Love that set the worlds to whirl in the void, is a stumpy Jewish guy tucking into his broiled fish and honeycomb?

Yes. No wise king nor visionary noble, no epic warrior nor brilliant merchant, no hero at all, no startling muscles, no beautiful visage causing women and men alike to swoon. Just a brown guy beaten by goons, spat upon in the street, hauled in for questioning by the cops, and trundled finally to the killing ground, one among millions forced at knife point to their deaths, shuffling along in chains and despair. A guy. A nobody. One of us. Us.

He was your testy brother, your wayward uncle, your troublesome cousin. He was your difficult son, your awkward neighbor, your unruly classmate, the guy who just didn't fit in, get with the program, go with the flow. We forget that. We forget he was us. We forget he was a jerk sometimes, snappish and surly, just like us. We forget he wept with fear at night, just like us. We forget he cried aloud in a terrible agony of loneliness, as every one of us has cried, in the bedroom, behind the barn, behind the chapel, in the back room of the bar.

And it came to pass, as he sat at meat with them, he took bread, and blessed it, and broke, and gave to them. And their eyes were opened, and they knew him.

They knew him by the breaking of the bread! And suddenly they recognized his hands, his face, his wry kind hawkish eyes; and they gave him a piece of broiled fish, and of a honeycomb, and he took it, and did eat before them, and almost certainly they ate with him, that very last time, and the bread tasted both sweet and bitter in their mouths, for they must have been stunned, and weary, and affrighted, and each in his heart knowing he was soon to leave them forever, until they saw him again by the right hand of the Father, in the unimaginable country made of love and joy; and he led them out as far as to Bethany, and he lifted up his hands, and blessed them. And it came to pass, while he blessed them, he was parted from them, and carried up into heaven. But a few hours later, I would guess, just after dusk, they sat again at table, those eleven men and surely several women, all of them both joyful and sore of heart, and they broke bread, and remembered him; and so do we all, every morning noon and night when we do the same, even unto this day; but remember ye the bruised witty dusty peculiar man he was; for it is by the very impossibility of who he was that we may yet be saved; we who are wholly human, but also shot through with the light of the Love.

Bird to Bird

When I was a child my grandmother withered over the course of some months until finally she was the size of a bird. In the end she was all bones and glare. She was a hawk one day and a gull another and a heron the next depending on the light. You would go to visit her and expect to see a gull like last time but instead there would be a disgruntled osprey in the bed. I pointed this out to my mother but she did not answer. Mom went every day. She took a different child with her every day. She would just look at one of us in a certain way when it was time to go and you would get in the car, mewling. The birds in Grandmother's bed made gentle mewling noises sometimes. Sometimes Grandmother cried without any sound. It is a loud silence when someone cries without any sound. She had lived with us for years. She was stern and forbidding and brooded in her perch like an eagle. Her spectacles flashed sometimes when she looked at you. Birds can see much further than people can. She could see through walls and around corners. She knew what you were doing before you did it. We would enter her room in the nursing home and Mom would say something gently and a falcon would open her eyes on the pillow. I wondered if the nurses knew that Grandmother could change form as she liked. Perhaps she could no longer control the changes and all day long she went from bird to bird under the sheets. That would be a tumult of birds. The nurses must have known but they probably loved birds and didn't say anything to anyone about it. Often Mom would say something gently and Grandmother would not open her eyes at all and Mom would just sit on the edge of the bed brooding and I would watch the bed for birds. Did she have a favorite bird to be? If you could be any bird would you be every bird or choose only one in which to live? Could you get stuck being a bird and forget that you were a person? Could the bird you wanted to be refuse you? Some questions you cannot ask anyone older. They will laugh or frown or give you advice. You have to just hold the question calmly in your hand and wait for the answers to come or not as they please. You cannot tell the birds what to do. The answer to a lot of questions is a bird. One time when Mom said something gently to Grandmother in the bed, an owl opened her eyes. Owls have piercing yellow eyes for which the words entrancing and alluring and riveting and commanding and terrifying were invented. Yellow is a dangerous color. Yellow means caution. Yellow means be careful and watch out and trouble ahead. Grandmother died very soon after that. You would not think a woman could wither into a heron but what do we know? Probably when Grandmother died the nurses picked up the heron gently and carefully and reverently in a towel and carried her outside, with prayers in their mouths, and they buried her under the sweetgum trees. Birds love sweetgum seeds. Probably whatever people thought Grandmother was is only a little of what she was. Surely we are made of more things than we know. We could be part goshawk, or languages no one knows anymore, or dreams a turtle had one winter under the ice. That could be. We went to Grandmother's wake because that is what our people did, and we went to the funeral because that is what our people did, but we did not go to the burial, because that is not what our people did, and also probably no one wanted to see the lean thin coffin in which you would bury a blue heron. Years later when I was driving past the nursing home where Grandmother died I thought maybe I would stop and poke under the sweetgum trees for heron bones, but then I drove on, because I like questions better than answers. Birds are how air answers questions. Birds are languages looking for speakers. Birds are dreams you can have only if you stay awake.

Mea Culpa

I laughed at gay people. I did. I snickered at their crewcuts and sashay and flagrancy. I snickered at the way they bristled about their rights. I did. I accused them of inventing disco. I laughed at their thing for feathers and glitter and fragrance and form-fitting uniforms. I grinned at the epic extravagance of gay pride parades. I laughed at the idea of gay guys battling cops hand-to-hand at Stonewall, noting snidely that *that* must have been a brief battle. Then I began to stop being such a meathead. Perhaps it was the sight of people weeping over the withering of those they loved with all their hearts and souls that snapped me awake. I stopped laughing. I started weeping too. The first time I saw the quilt I wept. The quilt is the biggest quilt you ever saw. It is more than a million square feet big. It is haunting and beautiful and terrible and lovely and bright and awful. Every panel is someone who died young. Every panel has tears in it. There are more tears in the quilt than there are threads. I started paying attention. I started listening. I stopped sneering and snickering. I began to hear the pummel of blows rained down on people for merely being who they were. How different is that from skin color and religion and ethnicity and nationality and the language that you speak? It is no different. I started listening. I heard stridency and silly demands and self-absorption and prickly neurosis but I also heard honesty and love and sense and logic and reason. If all men are created equal why do we not act that way? If all women are created equal why do we not act that way? If someone loves someone else what do I care what gender or orientation or identity they choose? If they want to spend their lives together in committed love, what do I care? The love of gay people for each other is a slippery slope to what, exactly? *More* committed love? Is that a bad thing? Is it a bad thing that couples wish to care for children when more children than ever before are without parents? How exactly is that a bad thing? Aren't two moms better than one? Who cares what gender the parents are? Isn't love bigger than gender? Also some people, a lot more than you would think, feel like they are born with the wrong body, and they switch bodies, and as far as I can tell they generally then are thrilled and comfortable and satisfied with their new bodies, and what do I care? This happened to a friend of mine, who spent thirty years as man, and then switched teams, and she has been a woman for fifty years, and you never met a more brilliant, generous, witty, gentle, wise, courteous, erudite, positive soul in your life. What is it exactly that is objectionable about her decision about her life? What do I care? What do *we* care? Where is there anything political in her decision? What sort of cold cruel arrogant religion would pronounce her decision sinful? Do not religions advocate love and mercy as the essential virtues? I have stopped sneering and snickering and laughing and teasing and making snide jokes about crewcuts and tight clothes and earrings. I was a fool. I was myself a joke, and not a good one. I said the words mercy and love and attentiveness and humility and tolerance and they were empty withered things in my mouth. No more. I am not gay. I am not bisexual. I am not lesbian. I am not transgender.

I am not questioning. I am generally delighted and thrilled and comfortable and deeply satisfied with my body and my gender and my identity, except for some disconcerting spinal issues. But I no longer think that my body type and gender and identity give me license to sneer at other types. I never thought being a pale brown color gave me license to sneer at people who were russet or bronze or copper or taupe or ebony in color; I never thought that being male gave me license to sneer at people who were female; I have stopped thinking that not being gay gives me license to sneer at people who are gay. It took me too long to stop thinking that, for which I apologize here, in the last lines of this essay. I have done many foolish things in this life, so far, and that was one of the most foolish, and cruel, and sinful. Mea culpa. Mea maxima culpa. Never again.

Fishing in the Pacific Northwest: a Note

Give a man a fish and you feed him for a day, goes the proverb attributed most hilariously to Maimonides, who wouldn't know a fishing pole if he woke up and found it murmuring alluringly in the bed with him, but teach a man to fish and you have bent his mind permanently toward hatching schedules, and caddis-fly casings, and the meticulous use of the pinion feathers of young hawks for complicated trout lures, and the epic grumpiness of mature salmon on their way upriver in pursuit of romantic entanglements in streambeds, and what the word *redd* means, and how to keep a sharp eye on osprey for which fish they are hauling out of the river and where they are hauling them from, and the intricate geometric wizardry of casting arcana, and exactly how long you should cache your bottles of ale in the creek for maximum chill, and how to identify poison oak, and where to find huckleberries near creeks and streams and rivers, and what color thread is best for which pool in which river, and when smelt run, and how to net them, and how to hate and detest and excoriate terns and cormorants for their incursions on the salmon population, and how to whip flat rocks on a line across a large river so as to clip a sea lion right behind the ear so as to drive him or her back down the river to the mouth of the river where he or she should properly be camping out and not this far upriver where you are fishing, and how to be startled when what you thought was a lean stick in the mud across the misty river suddenly takes wing and floats off upriver like a huge blue pterodactyl, and how to grin when a quartet of mergansers whips downriver like tiny intent feathered fighter jets, and how to notice the river accepting a mink without a splash, and how to distinguish otter tracks from raccoon tracks from muskrat tracks, and where deer and cougar and bear come down to drink and why that spot above all others is their favorite, and how not to jerk your rod when you feel an inquiry but wait patiently until the question goes to bold italic at which point contact is established and a relationship begun, and how to cradle the stunning creature gently while you disestablish contact, and how to savor the instant or two during which the creature holds, recovering his or her equilibrium, and then vanishes, with exactly the incredible effortless speed with which the bobcat vanished that time when you turned the corner of the trail and the bobcat turned the corner from the other side of the hill and the two of you stood there gaping for a second and then the bobcat just vanished without the slightest effort as if it has indeed evanesced, departed this wet and mountainous rock, slipped into another dimension, and perhaps reappearing amazingly in a grocery-store parking lot, if his or her gyroscope was slightly out of kilter that afternoon, much to the surprise of a small child with a balloon and a cinnamon-bun, who had reached down to pick up a gleaming nickel, but instead found herself staring into the endless amber mustard saffron golden bronze eyes of a bobcat, who stared back; and perhaps, maybe, it could be, it most certainly might be, that this mutual glance, this instant of utter absorption, set that child off on a life of attentiveness to the seething vegetative and mammalian and piscine and insectivorous and avian world around her, in ways that she might not otherwise have been stimulated to be; so it is, in the end, a very good thing, to teach a man, or a woman, or a child of any gender, to fish, as there is much more to be learned by fishing than how to catch fish; indeed how to catch fish is perhaps the least interesting thing about fishing, and there must be many people who go fishing not for fish but for something else altogether, so that when you ask them if they had a successful day fishing, and they say yes, but they have no fish, you know exactly what they mean, because you feel that way also.

On Not Giving the Kids Rides
in the Car Anymore

Which I hated, or thought I did, grumbling and mumbling and snarling and moaning and grumping and sighing o my gawd yet *again* I am supposed to drive someone somewhere and pick someone *else* up sometime later? Could you not get a ride from one of the other parents? Could you not ride your bicycle, or surf your otherwise ubiquitous longboard, or even, silly crazy talk, *walk?* Did the creator of the universe not issue you functional legs? How could a boy who plays basketball two hours a day, and sprints all day with his fellow ruffians, and dashes around the house and yard with the roaring dog, not have the wherewithal to walk half a mile to a friend's house? How could a girl who plays not one but two soccer games a day not be able to walk a quarter of a mile to her friend's house? Why is it unthinkable to propel yourselves using your natural locomotive devices, rather than haul the paterfamilias off the lovely couch?

But drive I did, and so did my lovely bride their mother, every blessed day for many years, twice a day, three times a day, sometimes more, all over town, dropping them off and picking them up, and picking up other kids and dropping them off, to the point where we knew pretty much every single cul-de-sac and shortcut and Drive and Avenue and Boulevard and Way and Trail and Street and Road and Circle and Court, and every bucolic development named Gardens or Terrace or Corners, in our town and close environs; and I knew every soccer field and basketball court and sprawling playground; and I knew where the cops camped out at night waiting for people to whiz down a hill ten miles over the speed limit; and I knew where each pothole was, and how deep and forbidding it was, and how long it had been there, and what depth it used to be before it achieved its terrifying maturity; and I knew which fast-food joints were open latest, and which ones to approach cautiously, wary of teenage drivers too confident of their skills after having their licenses for a few hours; and I knew where you might see raccoons and opossums at night, and where you might see deer, and the grassy field where, if you sat quietly for a few minutes before you were due to pick up a child, you might see owls sliding hugely through the dim mist, hunting for voles.

For all that I complained, and complain I did, vociferously and steadily and bitterly, I find that now I miss one thing, among the many things attendant and inherent in driving the kids to and fro: I miss them. I miss their lean length and their huge feet and their cheerful burble and the way they would slump drowsily back in their seats, smelling faintly of popcorn. I miss the fling of their backpacks in the trunk and the occasional wrestling of a bicycle into the car. I miss the clang of their longboards as they clunked them carelessly into the trunk. I even miss their silent intimidated friends calling me sir and mister, and the way kids would sometimes be crammed and crowded together when there were lots of them, and the way that occasionally one would sit on another's lap laughing and double-buckled even though this was inarguably illegal but we are certainly not going to mention this to your parents, are we? No, sir.

Now they are all away, and I drive alone in the car, mostly, except sometimes for my lovely bride their mother, or the dog; and while mostly I enjoy being alone, and being able to blast my music, and not hear piteous begging to pleeeease not play that old man music any more, there are times, I confess, when I glance in the mirror, and see no one grinning in the back seat, and my heart sags a little. Mostly then I turn the music up louder and carry on, but sometimes, here and there, for no reason, I'll say aloud *alright, where are we going this time, and what time do you want to be picked up? Just you, or are there other ruffians?*

Keeping Vigil

There are two chairs flanking Grandmother's bed and I am to sit in the chair by the window. That is the chair in which children sit and I am a child so. Grandmother is in the bed sleeping. I am keeping vigil. Mother says Grandmother is dying but she looks like she is sleeping to me. Grandmother is wearing her steel spectacles and they rise and decline very gently as she sleeps. When she dies Mother will remove her spectacles and we will give them to a child in Africa who needs spectacles and has never had spectacles but when he gets spectacles his whole world will change and that will be an act of goodness. If you do three acts of goodness Jesus stops what he is doing and glances over at you with a look of infinite tenderness. If you earn enough looks of infinite tenderness you can burn away your sins as if they had never been committed and not even Lucifer will know that you have sinned. Lucifer knows you sinned by the stench of sin upon you. The stench is on your soul, not your skin or your clothes. You can no longer buy off sins like you could in the old days. That was a mistaken custom and Martin Luther was correct to call Mother Church to task about that. He was a Catholic priest which we forget. So you can technically be Catholic and Lutheran, but only if you are Martin Luther. Grandmother said that and she was never wrong about anything because she spoke forcefully with conviction of her faith as a guide to her every thought and action. Grandmother says bad thoughts are sins. Mother says well now that is an amorphous area and we should be cautious about filling the boy's head with fearsome intimations. Intimations are hints and suggestions toward corporeal or substantive things. After Grandmother dies in this bed she will cease to be corporeal and will become utter spirit and we hope she will be returned unto the Lord from whom all things derive. I watch Grandmother's spectacles rise and decline and suddenly they stop and I am terrified and rather than call out for Mother I turn and keep vigil on the birds outside the window. There are two cardinals and one flicker. A flicker is a woodpecker although rarely will you see a flicker hammering away on a tree. Keeping vigil is a holy and unselfish act that each of us will do for one hour each during Grandmother's final hours. We are a family and that is what families do. You will keep vigil even if you do not want to keep vigil and no amount of whining and moaning and complaining and pleading will suffice. Grandmother suddenly gulps in a breath and I turn and look but she is still asleep. There is no clock in the room because if there is a clock in the room you will just stare at the clock rather than keep vigil over your own flesh and blood which is a holy and unselfish act recommended by the Church and surely something human beings have done since time immemorial. To keep vigil is to stand witness at the door between life and death. It is to acknowledge the imminence of death but stand guard over the holy soul of the loved one. It is ideally a time of deep spiritual meditation and not a time for recalling grudges and dwelling on unfortunate events in the past. It is a time of reconciliation and restoration, of quiet prayer for the soul of the dying person, that he or she be restored to the Lord from whom all things derive. Outside the window the flicker suddenly swoops on the cardinals and they scatter and the woodpecker begins to scarf up all the rest of the popcorn kernels that my sister scattered for the cardinals and my sister sprints out of the house roaring and waving at the flicker who flees. Just then my grandmother stops breathing again and I am afraid to turn and find her fled and a bad thought enters my head that her soul will become a flicker and gorge herself on popcorn kernels but Grandmother hauls in a breath again and my next brother comes into the room to relieve me and I am released; but to this day when I see a flicker I think of my grandmother, and I believe that those thoughts are prayers for her eternal soul, at home at last in the hand of the Lord.

The Bullet

Here's a story. A man who was a soldier in the American army in Iraq tells it to me. A friend of his, one of his best and closest friends, was nearly pierced through by a bullet fired by a sniper. The bullet entered the friend's upper right chest, just below the collarbone, and plowed almost through to the back, just below the shoulder blade. American surgeons removed the bullet and discovered it was a 5.56-millimeter cartridge manufactured in Lake City, Missouri. The Lake City Ammunition Plant was founded by the Remington Arms Company in 1941. Today it is operated by Orbital Alliant Techsystems, which averages five billion dollars in sales annually and earns an average of about half a billion dollars annually. Half of the one hundred biggest weapons and ammunition manufacturers in the world are American companies. Orbital is one of these. Orbital sells 1.5 billion rounds of ammunition a year to the American army and to the armies of other nations around the world. Some of that ammunition is lost or stolen or shuffled clandestinely to all sorts of revolutionaries, criminals, gangs, and thugs, including some which call themselves freedom fighters or insurgents against economic and cultural imperialism, though in many cases they are actually fighting to impose their own chosen form of oppression and tinny empire on the people they live among, people whom they are not averse to slaughtering for advertising reasons.

So let us review: an American soldier, age twenty-two, is nearly pierced by a bullet made in America, sold for a profit in

America, by an American company which makes half a billion dollars a year selling bullets and other weaponry to armies all over the world. The vast majority of the companies that make a tremendous profit every year selling bullets and other weaponry all over the world are American. Most of those companies are publicly traded companies in which many other Americans are heavily invested. So the bullet that nearly pierced an American boy, a bullet that caused him enormous pain, a bullet that permanently affected the use of his arm and shoulder, the bullet that cut a scar on his chest he will wear until the day he dies, was made in America, by American workers, and paid for by American investors, who profited handsomely by the sale of the bullet that eventually executed its purpose by punching a hole the size of a quarter almost all the way through a boy from America.

A 5.56 millimeter bullet can penetrate fifteen to twenty inches through "soft tissue"—soft tissue meaning, for example, a boy. The bullet is "prone to yaw," which means that it skews easily from a direct path, and it is also liable to fragment at what is called the cannelure, a groove around the cylinder. When a bullet fragments on delivery, the fragments slice and tear and rip and shred everything in their path, including bone. A 5.56 millimeter bullet can punch nearly half an inch into steel, and punch right through a bulletproof vest, and punch right through a human being of any size and shape and age and nationality and gender and religion and sexual orientation and combatant status, or not.

Rarely does a writer speak bluntly, ahead of time, to people who will type furious outraged insults in the comment section, after his article is posted, but I will here and now.

Dear outraged shrieking lunatic, you who are about to lecture me on how this was just an accident, and how it's a necessary part of the capitalist system, and how I am clearly a yellow liberal pansy: Are you only stupid, or are you insane? What part of all this makes sense? What part of all this is not about profit? Why should America be the biggest weapons dealer on earth? Why do we lie about how this stinks, and is directly linked to murders all over the world, and how our own kids suffer and die from American weapons and ammunition? Is profit share more important than the lives of uncountable thousands of people all over the world who die from our weapons and ammunition? There are no other products that all those American employees could possibly design and manufacture? Really? Have *you* ever been nearly pierced through by a 5.56 millimeter bullet? No? Then how do you have the unmitigated gall to say anything to me, you pompous ass?

The Courage of His Convictions

On the day my older brother was due at the draft board our father did not go to work. This was shocking. He always went to work. He never took a sick day. He barely took summer vacation. He rose early every morning and had toast and coffee and put on his fedora and walked through a thin scraggly forest to the train. But this morning he stayed at the table drinking coffee. This was startling. He was never at the table when we three youngest brothers were at the table mowing through breakfast before school. But there he was this day sitting companionably at the head of the table reading the paper. This was *The Long Island Press*, a broadsheet newspaper as big as a heron when its wings opened. As the oldest of the youngest brothers I spoke for us collectively when speaking for us three seemed necessary so I asked our father politely why he was at the table. My younger brothers listened silently. *I will be accompanying your brother to the draft board*, he said, from behind the heron's wings. We did not know what a draft board was. When our mother and our sister said the words *draft board* their voices were low and their faces tensed. Our brother had been in the Navy for one year of college and one summer during which he was on an aircraft carrier and sent us postcards. He never wrote more than ten words on the postcards. He was a terse gruff blunt brother who used words sparsely and pointedly and bluntly. He had no small talk, as our sister said. We did not know what small talk was either.

We thought it might mean talk that did not mean anything, like when people nattered outside church after Mass. The draft board was two towns away to the north. It was Local Board Number Four. When our sister said those four words you could hear the stern bristling dangerous capital letters. Those four words could send you to the war and the war could kill you. We saw the war on television and on the heron when it opened its wings. Our brother had quit the Navy. He did not think that shooting people was a sensible way to solve conflict. He is applying to be a Conscientious Objector, said our mother. We did not know what this meant. A boy down the street said that this meant our brother was a Yellow Belly Communist Coward and I punched him in the eye and his father stalked to our house and stood on our porch and shouted at our father and our father who never ever raised his voice loomed out onto the porch and spoke quietly but curtly and the other father stalked back down the street with a red face and our dad was grim the rest of that afternoon. Our dad had been in the United States Army in Not One But Two Wars, as our mother said, and it is a foolish silly soul who would dare speak to your father that way. Finally we had to go to school although we very much wanted to stay and watch our brother and our father drive off to Local Board Number Four, but no, off to school we went, slowly, looking back to see if the war would suddenly reach out and snatch our brother from the house. When we got home that afternoon our mother and father and brother and sister were all at the table even though it was not at all time to eat and we asked what happened and our father said he was very proud, very proud indeed, at the articulate courage of our brother, and he was proud that our brother had so taken the message of the Gospels to heart even at the cost of possible prison, and that we also ought to be proud of our brother, and if we three smaller brothers grew up to be as honest and courageous as our older brother he and my mother would be very proud, very proud. Our mother was weeping. Our brother sat silent. Our sister told us later that Local Board Number Four had been impressed that a veteran of the Second World War and the Korean War stood so proudly with his son as the son said that he refused to enter yet another war, because he believed violence was a terrible way to solve conflict, but that he, the son, would be honored to be of alternative service to the country he loved, which is why, said our sister, that our brother would be going away soon to be a teacher far away. Our mother said that we ought to be as kind to our older brother as we could in the days remaining to him in this house, and this we endeavored to do, for we loved him and he was our hero even though he was stern and gruff and blunt and had no small talk. Even before this all happened we wanted to grow up to be like him but after all this happened we wanted even more to grow up to be like him because now our father also thought that our brother was heroic because he had The Courage of His Convictions, and if you did not have The Courage of Your Convictions you were only an empty vessel, a hollow man, an insubstantial person, a soul filled with naught but wind, no more than a tinkling cymbal, tossed this way and that by the prevailing wind, of no measure or weight or character, and that is no way to be, boys, no way to be at all.

The Daoine Sídhe

When our daughter was little I left notes for her from the *daoine sídhe*, the small people, the people of peace, the hidden people, the people of the thickets. I left those notes everywhere outside the house, on the porch, on the path up to our house, on exposed rocks, gummed to the trunks of trees with sap, slipped into the clefts of bark, folded into the quadrants of the fence. The *daoine sídhe* are not easily seen but they are there in the bushes, in the mounds and hillocks of fields, flitting among the trees, smiling in the web and braid of branches. The notes were written on the shells and hulls of nuts and the flanks of leaves and the smooth bark of white walnut twigs. The *daoine sídhe* acknowledge that the world does not believe they are alive and well and adamant and elusive and interested in the doings of all beings of every sort and shape. I would try to leave a note every other day at least, and whenever I had to travel and miss a day or two of notes I felt a sag in my heart at the thought of our small daughter searching the porch and the fence and the walnut tree for notes and finding no notes and thinking perhaps the *daoine sídhe* were no longer her close and particular friends. There are many theories as to who the *daoine sídhe* are and one theory is that once they knew larger stronger crueler people were inarguably taking from them the places they loved they retreated to the shadows and the hidden places, under the ground and into the thickets, into all the half- seen half-noticed places all around us no matter where we live. We see so little. I would scrawl the notes with my left hand so that my handwriting could not be recognized and I was careful never to use a pen that she knew to be her father's pen. I learned not to leave notes from the *daoine sidhe* exposed to the rain because then the message would be washed away leaving nothing but hints and intimations. Sometimes I would leave a message without words. Another theory of the *daoine sidhe* is that they are supernatural beings but I do not think this is so. I think they are as natural and organic and present as you and me. I think that mostly what people think is supernatural isn't. I think there is much more going on than we are aware of and sensitive to and perceptive about, and the more we think we know what is possible and impossible the more we are foolish and arrogant and imprisoning ourselves in an idea. I think language is an attempt to drape words on things we sense but do not understand, like grace and the *daoine sidhe*. It is easy to say that the small people, the people of peace, the hidden people, do not exist, but you do not know that is so and neither do I. Our daughter used to write back to the *daoine sidhe* on the shells and hulls of nuts and the flanks of leaves and the nubs of cedar cones and on chips of bark. I kept every single note she ever wrote to the *daoine sidhe*. There came a time when I stopped writing the notes, because that time comes, and she stopped writing back, because that time comes, but there was a time when the *daoine sidhe* wrote to her, and she would rise from her bed, and run outside, and search the porch and the fence and the walnut tree for notes, and until the day I die I will remember the headlong eager way she ran, thrilled and antici-patory and delighted, with a warm secret in her face, because the people of peace were her friends, and they wrote her name on the skins of this world, and left her little gifts and presents, and asked her questions about her people and her dreams, and the bushes and hedges and thickets and branches for her were alive with mystery and affection, and to those who would say I misled our daughter, I filled her head with airy nonsense, I soaked her in useless legend and fable and myth, I lied to her about what is present and absent in the world, I would answer, And how do you know what is possible and impossible in this world of wonders beyond our ken? Are you really so sure there is not far more than you can see, living in the half- seen half-noticed places all around us? And to fill a child's heart with joy for any reason whatsoever, on any excuse whatsoever, for as long as howsoever possible, before the world builds fences and walls around her thrilled and fervid imagination, how is that a bad thing, how is that a bad thing at all?

Chessay

My son asked me to play chess yesterday. It was Easter. When a child asks you to play chess you say yes. He is twenty years old and an excellent chess player. I taught him to play when he was five years old. He first beat me when he was thirteen years old. What I remember best from that day is his slow smile when he and I realized, a few moves before the end, that he had toppled the king. I remember too that he did not crow or caper or shout or cackle but instead reached across the board and shook my hand, as I had taught him to do, out of respect for the game, and for your opponent, in whose mind you have been swimming for an hour. Chess at its best is a deeply intimate game in which you can delve into another person's mind and if you are lucky you get a glance a hint an intimation of your opponent's character and creativity, the cast of his mind, the flare of her personality, how he confronts difficulties, how rash or calm she is, how willing to be surprised, how well he loses, how poorly she wins.

He came out along his left wing, immediately establishing his knights, immediately forcing me to scuffle and skitter around on defense. My queen roared off her throne snarling and forced her way all the way to his back line but he deftly boxed her in with yapping pawns. Sometimes I think the pawn is the most powerful piece of all. Revolutions and religions begin with ragged beggars from the wilderness. I sent my bishops slicing here and there. My pawns grappled and died. He missed one golden fatal chance with a knight. The knight's curious sidelong move is the deepest genius of chess; it is the one piece that does not move in linear fashion, the one piece with a geometry of its own, the piece that goes its own way.

In a moment he will be thirty. I want to stare at him across the board for a week. He catches me in a mistake that takes me forever to redress. I don't know how to say any words that would catch the way I love him. I want him to outwit me. I want to win and I want to lose and I want to savor how deftly I am defeated. I often wonder if I have been a good enough father. A good father teaches his son how to kill the king. He makes an infinitesimal mistake and my rooks close in grimly. I have prayed desperately to die before he does. I would like to teach his children to play chess. I would like to show them how, if you are lucky, you can see inside your opponent, only occasionally, only dimly, only for a few minutes, but for those few minutes you get a hint an intimation a glance at who lives inside the castle of his body. What we see of each other is only a bit of who we are. I want to invent new words for what we mean when we say the word love. Chess can be a wonderful word for that. Chess is a lovely word that can't be spoken. After the game we shake hands and I think never in the history of the world was there ever a man happier to be a father than me. Never in the whole long bristling history of the world.

Laurel Street

One time years ago my wife and children and I were driving down a narrow dark road in my town. This is Laurel Street, which has a steep stretch with no lights, a stretch in which the road is pinched along a ledge between a perpendicular cliff and a precipitous bluff. A hundred times I warned our kids about that stretch, when they were biking and skateboarding and skittering free in our neighborhood; a thousand times I warned them about it again, when they began to drive the clan sedan; a dozen times I wrote to our civil servants, inquiring about the possibility of street lights, or reflective medallions, or *anything* in that tunnel; but that steep shadowy stretch of Laurel Street remains as narrow and dark today as it was that spring night years ago.

As I remember we were coming home from some burbling event at the elementary school, Field Day or Parent-Teacher Conferences or Graduation Night, and as I remember it was a russet spring evening, warm, the children happy and weary, jumbled like sweaty puppets in the back. Down the hill we drove, slowly, smiling at some joke, no one elbowing anyone for once, when suddenly there were high-beams behind me! and an idiot blaring his horn! and this just as I had entered the narrow dark chute on Laurel Street, in which a sensible driver slows down to a crawl and hugs the right side of the street, along the guard-rail, just in case some reckless fool comes roaring up the chute from below, probably not realizing that the street narrows, to the point where two cars can pass each other, but only by the slimmest of margins, really and truly two or three inches, if even that!

But this guy behind me is blaring his incredibly shrill strident horn, and racing his engine, and now he is *flashing* his high beams at me, and I am rattled and angry and fearful, and trying not to curse out loud, and wincing from his high beams in my mirrors, and squinting into the velvet dark to see how far we have left in the chute before I can inch even *further* over to let this jerk pass me, can he not see that *I have children in the car*, can he not wait another thirty seconds for us all to get out of the narrow dangerous chute?

And then, inconceivably, unbelievably, unthinkably, he guns his engine and passes us! In the chute! At about eighty miles an hour in a place where you should go ten miles an hour! And he is still leaning on his horn even as he passes us so narrowly I instinctively lean away and my shoulder touches my terrified wife's shoulder! And then he guns his car even faster and roars away at what I will later tell the police sure seemed like no kidding a hundred miles an hour! On a street with kids and dogs and bicyclists and old people out for their shuffling evening constitutionals while holding hands! And also speed bumps! I hope he hits that first speed bump and the entire chassis of his car falls off and he skids to a stop losing several layers of skin in the process!

I was so rattled that I stopped the car for a moment, after we got out of the chute, and we all checked on each other, and we were all still frightened. We drove slowly home, a matter of two minutes, and then I called the police. No, sir, I had not seen the license number, and no, sir, I was not sure of the make of the car, but yes, sir, I was all too sure of the speed and behavior of the driver, whoever he was. Somehow I knew it was a guy; something about the rage of his horn, the savagery of the way he passed us, the violence of his impatience.

The next day we heard what had happened after he blew past us in the chute. He had driven at more than a hundred miles an hour directly into traffic coming the other way. He died instantly. Somehow, incredibly, the other drivers were not seriously injured. He was young. Speculation was that he was drunk, on drugs, terribly depressed. He was young. Most of all I remember that he was young. I do not remember his name. For years what I remembered best was the powdery chalky bitter fear in my mouth as I pulled over after we came out of the chute. He could so easily have killed my wife and children. He could so easily have snuffed my children out of existence, in a heartbeat, in roaring flame and shrieking terror. I remembered my towering rage at such incredible arrogance and recklessness, such epic mismanagement of the torpedoes we drive so thoughtlessly, so casually, as if we have forgotten they are ferocious weapons, which we *have* forgotten, which we never think about, except in moments like that, and I am no different from you, and we should both be ashamed that we are so casual about the awful weapons into which we strap ourselves so carelessly every day, thinking about everything other than the terrible weapons we are about to set into motion.

But this morning I find myself remembering that he was young, and addled, and suicidal, and dark, and probably lonely, and probably frightened. He was someone's boy. Probably people loved him and feared that he was lost and feared that no rope or hand or word could reach him anymore. Probably he got in his car just about the time we piled into ours, and we set out for home, and he set out to die. I will always be furious about that haunted moment in the narrow chute, I will always feel a quiver of fear when I remember how close we came to death, but now I also feel a shiver of something else for that poor boy. The idiot who came within inches of killing my children was a rattled child himself. A good dad would pray somehow for that child, if all children are our children, which of course they are; and so yet again I have to try to find mercy inside pain, which is, as we both know, the work of a lifetime.

The Deceased

I measure the body with a ruler. The deceased is eight inches long and five inches wide if we count arm-span. There's not much in the way of arm-span. Mostly the arms are hands. The hands look eerily like baseball gloves. The teeth are tiny but populous and adamant. The tail is stubbish and not a tail you would boast about if you were in a pub and the talk turned to boasting about tails. It's more of a fleshy rudder than a tail. The eyes are small and black and open. I look in vain for ears. The nose is epic and tremendous and clearly what the face was designed to carry much like a ship carries a prow. I refrain from trying to ascertain gender, out of respect for the dignity of the deceased.

The deceased is, I believe, *Scapanus townsendii*, the Townsend's mole, native to this region, found everywhere from swampland to small mountains; but as soon as I read the parade of Latin labels by which it is classified, and wade through discussions of its economic impact on farm and pasture and garden, and former commercial value (coats and muffs and waistcoats made of mole fur were once popular, partly because mole fur has no 'grain,' as do other animal pelts), I begin to ponder the minimal substance of our labels and commentary on this and all other of our neighbors, and I wonder about this particular individual, and the flavor and tenor and yearning of this one life, and long I stand over its sprawled body, leaning on the shovel by which it will soon returned unto the earth that was its home and heart.

With sincere respect for Mr. John Townsend of Philadelphia, who wandered thoroughly in the forests and mountains of the West, paying such close attention to the beings therein that he is credited with 'discovering' plovers and swifts and warblers and thrashers and squirrels and bats and voles and chipmunks and this one tribe of mole, and who died young, merely forty-one, having slowly and unwittingly poisoned himself with the arsenic he used in preserving the animals he killed so as to study them more closely, I wonder what this particular mole at my feet called itself, or was called; how was it addressed, or thought of, or perceived, by its fellows? Was it a father, a grandfather, a great-great-grandfather? It is thought that this tribe of mole generally resides in home territories the size of a baseball field, and defends home court with remarkable ferocity, and that its children are generally born as spring begins, and that the children mature rapidly, and leave home as soon as they can, so that the family cavern, which is lined with a deep soft dense blanket of grass, and is accessible by as many as eleven tunnels running in every direction, is empty by the end of spring, and I stand here with the shovel thinking of the parents, proud of their progeny, but now bereft of their spirited company, and now alone in their echoing nest, busying themselves with quotidian duty; and soon this will be me, trying not to call our children every day, trying to celebrate their independence, trying not to wallow in memory.

This tribe of mole is thought to be largely solitary, I read, and I want to laugh and weep, as we are all largely solitary, and spend whole lifetimes digging tunnels toward each other, do we not? And sometimes we connect, thrilled and confused, sure and unsure at once, for a time, before the family cavern empties, or one among us does not come home at all, and faintly far away we hear the sound of the shovel.

I should toss the body over the fence, into the thicket, as food for the many, such being the language of life, but I think of how *we* feel when we are tucked tight in bed, inside the cocoon of the blankets, wrapped and rapt, and I wonder if moles love the grip of earth that way, love the press and dense of it, its inarguable weight, the blind swim through the dark, would love finally to dissolve in it; and I bury the body.

In Queens

Often we would drive to my uncle's house in Queens. Queens was in The City of New York. Queens was a Borough. There were Five Boroughs. Our father was from Queens and our mother was from The Bronx. The Bronx was upstate, near Canada. The Bronx was always referred to as The Bronx and not just Bronx. Why this was so was a mystery to us little kids in the back seat. We watched for the sign on the highway that said Welcome to The City of New York Robert F. Wagner Jr. Mayor, and once we were past it we were different. Even the starlings and pigeons along the highway were different. When we turned off the highway we stared hungrily from the windows of the car. There was graffiti and there were iron bars over the subterranean and first-floor windows of houses. There were chain-mail grilles and rattling metal doors pulled down over storefronts. There were old men smoking cigars in lawn chairs. There were young men with cans of beer. There were a great number of Oldsmobiles and Imperials. If we drove slowly enough past Springfield Park we could count languages and smell roasting meats and hope to see someone hit a home run. Our great dream was to catch a home run from the window of the car and then beg Dad to drive away hurriedly so that the outfielder would think there had been a miracle. The streets were lined by sycamore trees. Lawns were tiny and it seemed that every house was fenced. Time was slower in Queens. However late we had been while leaving our house we were never late when we got to our uncle's house. He was always sitting in the small dark comfortable living room listening to the radio. The voice on the radio was always a man murmuring in a low voice about Frank Sinatra or Louis Prima or Vic Damone. Our uncle would rise and greet our dad his brother and they would shake hands courteously and our uncle would bow to our mom because he was a Gentleman. He would lift an eyebrow to us which was his way of saying hello. He never met a word he couldn't deftly avoid, our dad said once. Our aunt his wife was Italian. She was in the kitchen with her mother who spoke no American. We said hello and clattered down to the basement where the food was. In Queens you could eat all day long and never grow weary of eating. In Queens there was cannelloni and ziti and lasagna and parmigiana and ravioli and cannoli and anise cookies in the colors of the Italian flag. There was garlic bread with so much garlic that people could smell you in Utah. The bread was hard outside and soft inside and once when I asked our aunt if she made her own bread she said why in heaven's name would I do that when there are five great bakeries within a mile? She smiled a lot and talked so fast we were not very sure of what she said. Our uncle smiled a lot and hardly spoke at all. The adults would all move to the tiny back yard spangled with sunlight falling down through the sycamore trees. They would sit in lawn chairs arranged in a circle. They would balance paper plates on their laps. In Queens everyone ate from paper plates. You could hear the Mets game from the radios from neighbors on either side. Sometimes both radios would have the Mets game at once and they would lose in stereo. No radio played the Yankee game. You could not be for the Yankees in Queens because that would be treason like Benedict Arnold who betrayed his friends which is a sin. Judas betrayed his friends. Judas would have played for the Yankees if he could have hit the curve, my uncle said once. Even our dad laughed at that and our dad was not much for the baseball, as he said. People who are not into sports use the word *the* before the name of the sport. We would leave at dusk and drive slowly back through Queens to the highway. If there was a sign that said You Are Now Leaving The Borough of Queens, I do not remember it. Usually our youngest brother would fall asleep and lean on us. Normally we would elbow him sharply awake because leaning is against the rules but he was the youngest and gentlest and we were tired and full of cannelloni and soon we were home and we would not be in Queens again for a while, although you could smell garlic and butter for days afterwards. Even now all these years later when I smell garlic and butter I think for an instant that I am in Queens.

The Sisters

There were the Sisters who taught grades one through eight: Sisters Aimee, Beatrice, Dorita, Everard, Gratia, Mary Margaret, Mary Therese, Rose Margaret, and Spiritu, the latter making it quite clear in the first minute of the first day of class that her name was not Spiritoo, or Spiritonto, or Spiritutu, or Sister Spiro Agnew, and any boy who muttered or jotted or scrawled a joke of that sort, and it was always a boy who did so, would regret that impulse for weeks afterward, and if any boy here did not believe Sister as regards this matter, he need only refer to his older brothers, if any, or the older boys in his neighborhood, of whom surely one or two remembered Sister Spiritu all too well, boys, all too well.

There were the Sisters who worked the convent: Sister Cook in the golden redolent kitchen, Sister Helen in the boiler room and garage and heating and cooling units, Sister Catherine in the office, Sister Blister the school nurse (real name: Sister Philomena), Sister Francine who ran the room in the convent to which women in the parish quietly came during the week and carried away bags of food and clothing and toys that had hardly been used at all and still mostly retained their sheen. If you paid close attention on Saturdays you could see a quiet procession of men delivering bags of food, and moms delivering bags of clothes and toys that had hardly been used, and occasionally a truck would pull up and unload whole gleaming crates of milk and cream. The driver was the dairyman himself, who was an inscrutable man; I asked him once about these deliveries to the convent and he said I do not know what you are talking about, which puzzled me.

There was Sister Eugenie, who dealt with the monsignor and the chancery, apparently as a sort of mediator or interlocutor; and Sister Teresa, who conducted site visits every four months, driving a 1959 Mercury Montclair four-door hardtop painted the color of sunsets in southern Utah; and once, only once that we ever remember, there was the Mother Superior, who was called Mother by the other sisters, although she must once have been Sister Something, which no one called her anymore; you wondered if she missed being a Sister, and sometimes wore Mother uncomfortably, like a wool mantle on a suddenly warm day.

Not one of them ever raped a child. Not one of them ever moved rapists from one parish to another without alerting anyone to the horror. Not one of them ever excommunicated or censured or silenced another member of their church. Not one of them ever played havoc with the pension fund or the endowment or the weekly collection. Not one of them ran off with a secretary. Not one of them ever instituted a formal investigation into the theological practice and beliefs of another. Not one of them publicly excoriated or insulted another member of their church for not believing exactly the accepted wisdom about ordination or contraception or the legitimacy of the Gospel of Thomas. Not one of them had a driver for her car, or a mitre for her head, or a summer palace outside Rome. Not one of them ever showed the slightest inclination, that I noticed, to worldly power and money and status and influence and fame.

As far as I could tell each of them, on a daily basis, embraced hard work, and kindness, and humility, and the idea that the Christ was resident in every heart, and that he should therefore be witnessed and celebrated in every person, and that anything that diluted or detracted from that work was selfish and small. As far as I could tell they were every bit as committed and dedicated to the ancient mission assigned by the Christ as any priest or brother or abbot or bishop or cardinal or pope, and, in general, collectively, less liable to ego, crime, scandal, and the hunger for secular power. So, I began to wonder as a boy, and still do, now more than ever before: why are they not in charge of our Church?

The Missing

There it is again in the newspaper this morning, on the radio, murmuring from the television, in bold type on the glowing screen in your hand: the haunted fraught awful phrase *the missing*. But it is wrong. It is inaccurate. There are no missing persons. No one is actually missing. They are just not where you thought they were, where they were expected to be, where they usually are, where they were last you looked, where they always are, unless something is wrong, usually something small, but not this time, not this time.

But they are not missing. They are right there, under the wreckage, the detritus, the crumbled infrastructure, the fallen highway, the shivered ruins. They are sprawled, supine, curled, crumpled, battered, bent, broken. Shockingly often they seem serene. Very often they seem sound asleep under their masks of dust and chalk and riven stone.

They are not missing, though: only unfound. In a day or five or ten they will be uncovered, discovered. Pulled from, hauled from. The towers collapsed, the earthquake rumbled, the tornado tore, the battle burst like a boil, the hurricane lashed and flooded. Words lose their meaning in the roaring. Words are shredded. Words are whipped by the terrible wind. She should be coming through the back door just about now, rude and grumpy, *peevish and peckish*, as her grandfather would say, he loves those words, *peevish and puckish and peckish*, he has often draped those words on her, wrapped them about her

testy perfect face like a scarf or a shroud, and the dog as usual
is listening for the faintest possible scuffle and skitter of her feet
in the gravel at the top of the hill, and the doorknob is hungry
for her hand, but now the door will starve for that hand for
the rest of its days, for she is among the missing, the missing
who are not missing, but only flailed, felled, fallen. Their souls
have fled their bodies. Who they were no longer abides in what
they were. Who they were is loosed and lost. Now when you
say her name you are in the past tense, in the tense past. It used
to be that her name went with her like a handle or a shadow
and now it is without, unattached, whirled in the wind. The
dog waited by the door for more than four hours, despite every
instruction and command to abandon his post. Only long
after darkness fell did he cease to stand and wait, to attend, to
watch, to expect and savor the exquisite and idiosyncratic joy
of her presence.

A Mohawk in the House

One time when my twin sons were small, and we three were on our own for a few days, as their mom and sister were away, we decided that the boys should have their hair cut by Dad, because Dad thought he could do roughly as good a job as the professional, and if Dad did the barbering then the boys could have the five bucks each that Dad would have spent on the professional, so the boys, avid for cash, totally bought in to the idea, and the dad was totally invested, thinking how hard could cutting four-year-old hair be?

So out we went into the yard with a chair and a scissors and light hearts.

It turned out to be harder than I thought, because the chair wobbled in the uncertain grass, and the boy in the chair wriggled, and his twin bounced around distractedly, causing more wriggling, and the birds came down from their sylvan parapets to watch, including a varied thrush, which you hardly ever see, and an inquisitive squirrel inched down the cedar tree, which excited the dog, which caused more wriggling, and I made a major surgical error with half the hair of the boy in the chair.

We paused to take stock of the situation.

Essentially it was a disaster—the boy in the chair now looked like someone from a preening insipid Eighties mullet band—and there was nothing to do but try to balance the mistake with radical surgery on the other side. After that, though, his hair fore and aft stuck out like he had a tiny surfboard in his hair, so I cut all that off too, and tried to even out the remaining vegetative growth, with some success, although now his head looked eerily like the lawn, in which some patches grew furiously and others reluctantly, but by now the boy in the chair was restless beyond endurance, and his twin brother was itching for *his* turn, so they traded places, and the whole unfortunate story played out again, as if, even though I had quite clearly remembered the past, I was condemned to repeat it, at least upon the pate of my next son, who swiftly looked like Joe Strummer in his brief Mohawk period, which set his twin brother to laughing so hard he fell down, and got twigs in his hair.

I was awfully tempted to leave the Mohawk on my son, because *he* was cool with it, knowing it would awe the neighbor children and annoy his older sister, and because you hardly ever see a four-year-old with a major Mohawk, and because even the *word* Mohawk is cool, honoring the Bear People of what was for many years the great Iroquois Confederacy of eastern America, in which the Mohawk were the Keepers of the Eastern Door against invaders from east and south. Also his twin brother was cool with it, because having a brother with a towering Mohawk makes *you* cool by association, and also we had two days yet before the mother and the sister were due back from gallivanting, so finally we took a vote, and weighed pros and cons like sensible men, and decided that as it was Sunday he could keep his Mohawk all day long, but that I would snip it before he went to bed, and this we did that night, on the porch, right after I handed each boy a crisp five-dollar bill, as promised.

All in all this was a pretty good day, as the non-Mohawk twin said to me sleepily, after I finished telling the boys stories and tucking them in. *We saw a thrush, and there was a Mohawk in the house.* Even now, all these years later, that last seems like a particularly lovely sentence to me, one that I will always be happy I heard.

Selections from Letters and
Comments on My Writing

Why do you abuse punctuation so? What has punctuation ever done to you? Where were you educated, if you *were* educated? Did you not study grammar? Breaking all the rules of syntax, apparently deliberately, does *not* constitute art. The fur-trapper in your novel is an evil man and a liar and you should be ashamed of yourself. Why are there no dogs in your novel? Do you have something against dogs? How can a man write an entire novel about a town and not mention a single dog? In several of your essays you say that cats are the brooding spawn of Satan. Why do you say such things? Are you trying to be funny? I will assume that you are trying to be humorous but it certainly is not amusing to us in the cat community. In your book about a vineyard you refer constantly to your lovely research assistant. I just discovered from the Web that you are married, and have been married for many years. Does your wife know about your research assistant? In your book about a vineyard you veer off every other chapter into whatever seems to be in your head at that time. Why did your publisher let that happen? Our book club read this book and we got into such an argument about it being inane or brilliant that the book club was dissolved and now I have to find a new book club, for which I blame the author. In your novel about seafaring there is a mistake on page 211. In your novel about a pine marten there is a mistake on page 208. In your novel about the Oregon coast there may be a mistake on page one, second paragraph, but your writing style is so weird that it may not be a mistake. I find your ostensibly 'spiritual' essays to be nothing more than religious claptrap deviously designed to sell the scurrilous agenda of the Papist Church. Your nominally 'spiritual' essays should bear a large warning sticker on the cover warning sensible and reasonable readers to stay away. I have now read all three of the books that you claim are 'poetry' but not one of them is anything near as good as Mary Oliver ever wrote. (To that reader I wrote back, agreeing with her wholeheartedly.) Why do you not use quotation marks in your novels? Our book club just read your novel and one of our members pointed out that there are no adverbs in the entire book. Did you do that on purpose or was that an accident? I have to write a paper about your writing and when I go to Wikipedia it says you were born in 1935 and 1956. How is that possible? Is that because you are Canadian? Our class is studying your essay about hummingbirds and we do not understand the ending. Do you? Our class read your book about hearts and when our teacher asked *What was he thinking?* we were all thinking exactly that. Our book club had to read your novel for our April meeting and my question to you is this: who were you trying to ape and copy, James Joyce or Jorge Luis Borges? Please respond to this question: I have ten dollars riding on Borges.

The Third Order of Saint Francis: a Note

When I was perhaps ten years old my mother and father, devout Catholics who sought a deeper and more intimate spiritual experience than just their parish life, began attending meetings of the Third Order of Saint Francis, one of the many tertiary clans in the Church; the first two Orders being men and women who have sworn vows and belong to one of Catholicism's many congregations of priests, monks, brothers, and sisters.

As regards the actual tenets of the Third Order of Saint Francis, and the depth and length of my parents' commitment to it, and exactly where and how long my younger brothers and I went with my mother and father to the meetings, I have not a clue, although I can guess that simplicity and service were the watchwords of the day, what with that most admirable man Francis's name engraved on the enterprise. But it is not the Order and its long history that fascinates me this morning; it is the fact that my mom and dad, then in their forties, working furiously to house and feed and protect and educate and elevate their many children, would happily add two or three hours to their duties every week or two, simply to go deeper into their faith.

We would drive to some unfamiliar church or school, two or three towns away, and make our way to the basement—always it was a basement, as if returning in spirit to the catacombs in which the Christian cult began so long ago—and there we would part, our parents into the meeting, and us boys into the nether chambers of the unfamiliar school. Often we would be nominally stationed in the library, or a classroom, where we would wait decorously until we were sure the meeting was up and running, at which point we would slip away to explore; I suppose my brothers and I ranged more freely in Catholic schools on Long Island than any other boys we knew, voyaging through teachers' break rooms, and principals' offices, and janitorial storerooms, and fraught haunted chapels, and even the occasional low-ceilinged gymnasium, where the floors shone alluringly, and we skated hilariously and silently in our socks.

Those dusty school basements, with their ubiquitous scents of stale coffee and linoleum wax and unknown schoolchildren; the clank and clatter of metal folding chairs, ever so slightly rusted, and never to be oiled in this life; the fat plastic smell of day-old doughnuts and the big buttery boxes in which they rattled; the beam and heft of the occasional Franciscan friar, and the wisp and grin of the occasional Franciscan nun; the hat-racks on which the men hung their fedoras and Irish caps, and the coatracks on which the women carefully draped their raincoats and lovely pastel overcoats; the motley other Third Order children we studiously avoided, as we ranged about the unfamiliar school, free and independent for exactly as long as the meeting lasted; I remember this all now faintly and clearly at once, all vague and sepia and almost forgotten except for a sudden crisp detail—skating in our socks!

For many years the sort of writer I was would revel and relish in those details, and tease them out, and so defeat time, reclaim some of the existence we are so sure is lost with age; but now the sort of writer I am is staring not at the happy footloose boys but the weary gentle parents. A woman and a man in their forties, avid and energetic members of their parish, with one small income between them, with four children in Catholic school and one more on the way, regularly surrender three hours of their weekend, so that they may more deeply explore a faith devoted to the revolutionary idea that Christ is resident in every heart, that miracles are not only possible but prevalent and accessible, that every living being is evidence of grace, and that every being, in a real sense, is potentially a priest, standing as awed witness and celebrant of divine love loose in this world. They took their faith so seriously, so happily, so thoroughly, so deeply, not merely as religion, but as compass point and lodestar, that I find I cannot take it any less seriously, not if I love and revere them, as I do.

Whenever I grow dark about my Church, and go gray at the gills about its addiction to power and greed, its corporate smirk about the lost and helpless, the very souls it was created to succor, I remember my mother and father herding us three youngest boys into the station wagon, on a Sunday afternoon, when we would have rather done anything else in the world except drive two towns over to the Third Order of Saint Francis meeting. Perhaps they too drove to the meeting a bit reluctantly, half-wishing they could stay home and nap, or garden, or watch the game, or repair the storm windows, or read Ernie Pyle in the hammock, but they went. Probably the best lessons we teach our children are not the ones for which we use words; perhaps those are the lessons the children never forget. As you see.

To the Beach

One time for no reason at all my kid brother and I decided to ride our bicycles from our small brick house all the way to the beach. We got maps out of the family car and pored over them and concluded that it was about four miles to the beach. He was twelve and I was thirteen. We could cut through a few neighborhoods before we had to thrash through the grass along the shoulder of the highway. The shoulder of the highway would be a problem because twice the highway crossed bridges over the tide flats and we would have to dismount and balance along the curb by the rail where there were only about six inches of play. We figured we would worry about this when we came to it. We supplied ourselves with cans of soda and two sandwiches each and one beach towel each. We debated about the surfboard. What if it was windy along the highway and the board caught a gust and one of us was obliterated by a truck? Mom would be mad and the surviving son would be sent to his room for life and never again see the light of day and wither away pale and disconsolate like Edgar Allan Poe. But we tested the wind with our fingers and it didn't seem too bad so we brought the board. The board was five feet long and fatter than it should have been. We worked on that board every day during the summer with wax and affection and dreams of glory. However the board was obstreperous and no matter what we did the bicycles adamantly refused to carry it. Finally we decided to carry it between us and in this ungainly manner we set off for the beach. For a while all was well except for the amazed looks of passersby and the occasional ostensibly witty remark. Why people try to be witty on the spur of the moment when the only people available to hear their ostensibly witty remarks are the very people they are trying unsuccessfully to be witty *about* is a mystery to me. Finally we had to climb the embankment up to the highway and head south to the beach. Just then my brother reminded me that we would have to pass the toll booth through which the highway funneled so that Robert Moses could recoup the money he had spent providing Jones Beach as a gift to the people of New York State. We decided that we would worry about this when we came to it. By now we were weary and the surfboard was incredibly heavy so we stopped and ate a sandwich as the cars whizzed by and one car threw a beer can at us for no reason we could tell. Because we were both reading the Hardy Boys at that time and wanted to be detectives we instantly looked for the license plate and my brother who had a ferocious memory memorized it and also wrote it in the sand just in case. We proceeded on. There were now flies and mosquitoes but also there were rabbits at the foot of the wall of bushes along the shoulder of the highway. We came to the first bridge and after a brief meeting decided that we would walk the bicycles one by one along the curb and then come back for the surfboard. A guy slowed down to help us or rob us as we were walking the surfboard over but we waved him on impatiently using the glowering faces we admired on construction workers and our older brother who worked at the tollbooth up ahead. We used the same plan at the second bridge although this time a gust of wind did come up and we almost were blown into the highway just as a truck roared past and we were almost obliterated and we made a deep and secret pact to never ever tell our parents about this incident, a pact I am reluctant to break even now. This experience made us hungry so we ate our other sandwich and drank our sodas and buried the cans in the sand for archeologists to find in the 27th century after Christ. We proceeded on. The highway led inevitably to the tollbooth and for the first time we noticed that there was no way around the tollbooth without being seen from the state police office; Robert Moses was no fool. As our mother said you had to admire the devious energy of the man even though he was an arrogant tyrant who should be in prison for destroying a thousand neighborhoods and their vibrant cultural fabric. By now we were exhausted and hot and thirsty and both of us would have cried if the other was not there. We sat for a few moments reconnoitering and then my kid brother to my amazement walked right up to the toll booth and knocked on our older brother's window and a few minutes later our older brother drove over in a battered gray truck and put us and our bicycles and our surfboard in the truck and took us to West End Two, which was and probably still is the best beach for surfing, and we surfed there for the rest of the afternoon, not very well, until the end of our older brother's shift, at which point he came to get us in his Ford Falcon, and carried us home. On the way home we were so tired that we both fell asleep together in the tiny back seat. We were so tired that we stayed asleep even when we got home and our older brother quietly unloaded our bicycles and the surfboard and put everything in the garage. I had woken groggily when he closed the trunk of the Falcon and I remember seeing him with one hand on each bicycle and the surfboard under his arm as he walked to the garage. Even today all these years later when I think of our older brother that's one of the first things I remember. You would think that I would remember him in his tuxedo on the day he was married, or in his flowing academic robe on the day he earned his doctorate, or hoisting up his kids delightedly like tiny loaves of bread on the days that they were born, or even gaunt and grinning in the weeks before he died, but no, it is him tall and thin and silent at dusk as he walked our bicycles and our surfboard back to the garage that I remember the most. The things that we remember the best, the things that matter the most to us when we remember them, are the slightest things, by the measurement of the world; but they are not slight at all. They are so huge and crucial and holy that we do not yet have words big enough to fit them, and have to resort to hints and intimations to even get anywhere close.

Huddle

We did do atom bomb safety drills in grade school. We did. No one today can believe that kids actually practiced huddling under their desks or huddling in the hallway but indeed we did practice huddling in places that even then we knew would not protect us at all in the least.

We could talk for a while about how crazy this was, to practice huddling, and how silly it was for figures of authority who surely knew that we would all be roasted instantly no matter how well we huddled to insist in no uncertain terms that we practice huddling, or even get annoyed when some kids did not huddle very seriously or silently, and actually no kidding mete out punishment for kids who were not huddling at all, but I would rather consider the actual act of huddling, because rarely do we think about huddling, not to mention collective huddling, and huddling in straight lines, and huddling by gender and age, all of which we did, some years ago, in grade school, not far from the very ocean over which the atom bombs would travel.

I don't know about your school's atom bomb drill, but our school's atom bomb drill began with a crackling announcement over the public address system, and as soon as we heard the words *bomb drill* we were required to kneel under our desks and huddle with your head between your knees, resting either on your forearms or on the cold linoleum floor, your choice. No, you could not squat, and no, you could not sit cross-legged, and no, you could not curl up as if you were taking a nap, and no, you could not sprawl supine with your legs poking into the boy huddled under his desk in front of you. Unbelievably there was a proper position in which to huddle during atom bomb drill, and that position was enforced by our teacher, who twice that I remember patrolled the aisles correcting huddling form and kneeling down herself to exhibit proper form for those children who were just not getting the idea.

If by chance you were not in your classroom when the public address system crackled with the principal's grim voice saying the grim words *bomb drill*, you were required to huddle along the walls of the hallway. No, you cannot huddle in the bathroom. If you are in the bathroom when you hear the words bomb drill, walk, do not run, walk out into the hallway and join your classmates in huddling along the walls of the hallway. If you cannot immediately find your classmates, huddle with whatever students of whatever age are huddled along the walls of the hallway. Older students will make an effort to be attentive to younger students, who may be frightened, and should be calmed gently. If by chance you are outside the school when you hear the words *bomb drill* you are to huddle along the nearest walls, be they the walls of the school, the convent, or the rectory. Do not leave the school grounds under any circumstances. Avoid open areas. Again older students should pay special attention to younger students, who may be frightened, and should be calmed gently.

Never that I remember did any student or teacher or janitor or secretary or librarian or nurse or assistant principal or principal or pastor discuss geopolitics, or the morality of war, or the actual physics of being roasted instantly. We just huddled when it was time to huddle. I am sure that there is much to be said about the lies of our leaders, and the hypocritical demonization of the Other, and our own national culpability in roasting enemy cities, but here at the end of the page I just want to remember the rustle and scuffle of children huddling under their desks and in the hallways and out along the walls of the rectory, the almost-silence, the thrill and the fear, the whispers, the snickers, the ache of your knees, the cold baptism of the linoleum floor, the deep private squirm of terror that this time it was not a drill and never again in this life would you see those you loved. A moment later the public address system crackled again and we stood up and that was that. You can say that we never were bombed, and you would be right, but how many children carry scars from all those moments when they huddled with their heads between their knees? No one ever talks about that, do they? We laugh about the idiocy of atom bomb drills in the old days, because of course huddling was stupid and each child and desk and stone and teacher and wall and roof and crucifix would be vaporized instantly, but it isn't actually funny at all, is it? Millions of children carry those hidden scars. We never talk about hidden scars like that but maybe sometimes we should, just for a moment, like now.

Dressing for Mass

It is not now the fashion to dress meticulously for Mass, and I cannot say that I completely mourn the old custom, for it is inarguably more comfortable to wear khaki pants and my Saturday Dad Doing the Errands Jacket than a suit; but on days when I see young men wearing surfing shorts to Mass, I find myself drifting back to the hour before Mass when I was a boy, many years ago, in a large family, which featured many boys, but only one girl, which was a fortunate state of affairs on Sunday morning, for my sister would claim the bathroom like a disputed territory long before dawn, and marinate in there for hours, apparently addressing each of her many long hairs by name, and cooing to it lovingly, and asking it gently about its emotional state, and taking eight or nine baths and showers alternately, while snarling terrifying imprecations at her brothers, who hammered on the door so assiduously that our dad twice had to putty over the places where his sons had thrummed on the door, begging in the most polite and courteous tones for just one moment of ablution, shy murmured requests that were denied with the most shocking and vulgar language, and this before we were to go to Mass and sit silently and ponder the Unimaginable Mercy at the root of all things, even our sister.

Occasionally we would try to beat our sister to the bathroom early, just to snatch the briefest of showers, even though she would vengefully run the kitchen tap in an effort to scald us out, but mostly we just lay abed until the last possible second, and then we dressed and thundered downstairs for shards of toast before being packed like herrings in a light olive oil into the car by our dad, who always wanted to strap our youngest brother atop the car for entertainment's sake, saying *What do we have ski racks for if not for strapping Tommy to the roof of the car?* Tommy was willing, I should say, and we were all willing, but our mother was not willing, and our sister never weighed in on this because she was still in the bathroom applying her final mysterious unguents and potions. Every single time we ever went to Sunday Mass as a family my father would start the car, as the first signal to our sister that we were indeed leaving without her, and then he would turn the car around, as a second signal, and then he would bleat the horn, as a third signal, and then he would let the car inch forward slightly, which was the last straw, at which point our sister would come pelting out of the house like a fragrant harpy, trailing clouds of unguent and bad attitude.

For some years three of us boys lived upstairs together, and we would dress together by the old mirror, putting on the suits our mother had laid out for us, the suits we wore only for Mass and weddings and wakes, the suits we thus assumed were made of sacramental cloth. The crisp white shirts, sometimes still warm from our mother's steam-iron; the ties of various hues handed down by our father (fat ties) and older brother (narrow ties); the black shoes, polished by your breath and a brother's stolen sock; the utilitarian unfashionable black belts issued to all American male children at birth; the crisply ironed white handkerchief that each male in our clan carried by command of our mom, who grimly lined us up by the front door and checked for clean handkerchiefs before we were allowed out into the soiled world. Showers not being part of the program, what with our sister camped out in the bathroom since Tuesday, we did what we could to tamp down the unruly thickets of our hair; and more than once, I now confess, we tamed our youngest brother's hair with the spit that God had seen fit to grant us as part of the amazing salivary system, without which you could not properly eat or digest your food.

It took time to get dressed for Mass; our poor mother ironed everything in sight for hours, preparing us for public inspection; and yes, there were times than we moaned and whimpered and complained about the custom, whining and mooing like pro soccer players. Yet even now that I am long past the habit of dressing in my best for Mass, I sometimes feel that I should, and not just for nostalgic reasons, or to hint to the boy with surfer shorts that he ought to get a grip. No; it has something mysteriously to do with respect, and humility, and ritual, and reverence. When I was young I thought dressing for Mass was silly and empty performance art; now I wonder if it was more a gesture of something like awe. For great moments in life you prepare slowly and carefully, and present yourself buffed and polished and shining, as a way to say something for which we do not yet have particularly good words.

A Note on Scapulars

My grandmother wore one. My lovely bride wears one. I carry one in my shirt pocket. Once they were almost ubiquitous in the Catholic world, so common that I would see them peeking from the necks of aunts and uncles, dangling from the necks of men changing their shirts in sacristies and locker rooms, draped on the chests of men and women in their gleaming coffins at their wakes and vigils and viewings. But now even the word *scapular* is a rare sighting, let alone the lovely gentle honest thing itself; so let us spend a moment celebrating and honoring the scapular, a small subtle savory spiritual whisper that moves me whenever I encounter it.

Probably they trace their history to monastic robes—many monks and nuns to this day wear a front-and-back cloth, something like a narrow poncho, called a monastic scapular; Cistercian friends of mine wear them regularly, and often use them as de-facto aprons in their work in the book-bindery, the kitchen, and the carpentry shop of their abbey. The much smaller scapular that laypeople wear—essentially two stamp-sized squares, usually of cloth, attached by strings, and worn such that you carry a square on your chest and on your back— probably began as a gesture of affiliation with a monastery, abbey, or order; while you yourself were not, for example, a Trappist monk, you admired the graceful men who were, and you wore a token of that esteem, as an act of witness and of prayer. In general scapulars come in one of five colors, each associated with a particular devotion or saint; my lovely bride carries Our Lady of Mount Carmel with her every day, because she and Our Lady are close confidants, being mothers and women of grace and courage. I take a special pleasure in seeing this particular scapular here and there, in the rare moments when it does not adorn the woman who married me, for I like the fact that Mount Carmel, in Israel, is called 'God's Vineyard' in Hebrew, and is a holy place for the Baha'i, Jewish, and Muslim faiths as well as for the Christian faith; indeed it is thought to have been a sacred place long before any of those religions existed, which cheers me up, for it reminds me that holiness is bigger than any religion, and that what is sacred cannot be owned or controlled or claimed by any one religion or people or sect or species.

There is holiness, bigger than even our capacious imaginations can reach, and then there are countless religions and faiths and traditions, each striving, at its best, to witness and celebrate and honor the gift of holiness in this world; and one way that religions witness and celebrate and honor the sacred is with the humble gestures of cloth and metal and wood, glass and stone and shell, paper and smoke, water and wine. The little tactile things that we do and wear and touch, the rosary beads and medals engraved with the faces of the saintly, the chalice and the host, the missal and the ashes, the crucifix and the cross, the mantilla and the scapular...how easy to sneer at them as devotional mania or simple-minded superstition, but how anciently and deeply human and humble, to see them as things we can daily touch and see and smell, to remind us of that which is far beyond our poor dim senses. We can, if our eyes be open and our minds clear, see and hear and touch the evidence of holiness everywhere, flung with the most amazing profusion, babies and bears, trees and tenderness, water and laughter, forgiveness and mercy, the very air we breathe, the very lungs with which we breathe it; we can, in short, see the fingerprints, and hear the echo, and trace the spoor, the trail, the signs; and then, with something like awe, we can finger such prosaic things as rosaries and scapulars, and so silently speak and sing and shout our gratitude; and then you slip your scapular gently back into your shirt, and proceed into the next holy hour granted you by a most generous and profligate and incomprehensible Love.

Our Rough Uncles

Spent an hour with a three-year-old kid last night, talking about bears, and was again reminded that the purest of people is a three-year-old kid. Gender makes no difference, as far as I can tell. They *focus*, you know? If they like bears, you are into bears for the foreseeable future, and nothing gets in the way of bears. And it turns out there are a lot of things you can talk about when you talk about bears. There are bears *of all sorts of colors*, probably more colors than we have words for colors, when you think about it, because bears have been around longer than words have been around. Bears have been around since before there were even *pencils*, as my young friend said, which is a remarkable sentence, and inarguably true, and not something I had ever considered before. He drew some bears, with a pencil, to show me the sort of bears he was talking about, which looked roughly like black bears. I told him I once saw a black bear in Canada, on the side of a mountain near a glacier, and we talked about all this for a while, the ideas of Canada and glaciers being new to him, but not mountains, *he* knew mountains, mountains were in his *dreams*, where they *spoke* to him, they have deep voices, like bears. This was another new idea for me, that mountains and bears might have similar voices, probably from being around each other for many millions of years. I mentioned that in my reading I had once discovered that bears appear to have been around for about forty million years and probably began quite small, about the size of your dog, but then over the years some species got to be whopping huge, and we agreed that this was pretty cool, and drew some more bears for a while, before he decided that running one million laps around the house was a good idea, and away he went.

I thought about bears on the way home, and how when we are children we feel a certain friendship and camaraderie generally with bears, partly because of the whole teddy-bear thing, but also because they are large and hairy and independent and strong and no one messes with them, as a rule. I wonder if part of the reason we so like bears when we are young is because we would like to *be* like bears, eating anything we want and sleeping where we want and not being told what to do by anyone. It is interesting how often bears appear in an avuncular capacity in our modern stories and myths and fables, often acting as powerful and exacting but fair-minded mentors to young avatars like Mowgli and Lyra and Frodo. Have bears changed their roles in our stories over the last thousand years, from grim implacable avatars of wilderness to be defeated and conquered, to rough uncles, grandfathers who seem stern but are not so stern at all, older brothers who are actually gentle beneath their mountainous muscles? Once a youth would go into the wilderness and test his or her mettle against the biggest and wildest resident therein; could it be that now that there is no wilderness, there are no longer those sorts of bears in our dreams?

When we talk about all that is lost in a world in which wilderness is lost, we rightly talk about the species a day that vanishes forever, and the holiness of that lost life, and the dwindling possibility that new species will emerge if there are no wild places in which they might be born, and the terrible possibility that the new organisms that may be born are those against which we have no defense, like viruses immune to our medical maneuvers and manipulations. But we never really talk about the loss of the life we *imagine*, the life that speaks to us in deep voices in our dreams. When there are no bears in the world, then no children will dream of bears, and draw bears, and sleep with bears, and that will be a terrible shame. That will be a sin, to call a thing by its true name.

Infans Lepus

I t's his nature, we say to the kids when the dog catches and kills an infant rabbit. It's what he was designed for. There's no blame to assign. Millions of years of training. Survival instinct. Prey response. Scent trail. An ancient relationship, really, between the Canidae and the Leporidae. Each exquisitely aware of the other. Probably the rabbits evolved the predilection toward large litters in part because of pressure from the Canidae. Themselves descended from a common ancestor of the felids also. Thus the ancient enmity there—a fraternal thing, the same strange nonsensical hate that religions have for each other, though they claim the same target and inspiration. Is this too much information? I am trying to soften the blow of the shredded bloody scrap of rabbit. The size of my fist. If that. Bedraggled. So recently alive and promising and tiny and almost certainly loved, if we can use a word like love with creatures we do not know very well, in the end. We know a great deal about the shape and manner and pace and rhythm and exterior of their lives, but of their real lives, their interior lives, their emotional lives, their spiritual lives, their musings, their sensory illuminations far beyond our abilities, we know, well, do we really know anything? We can say with some assurance that this particular rabbit had a father and a mother, and almost certainly brothers and sisters; were we to pursue the matter we could probably find the natal nest in the blackberry thickets, did we steel against the pricks; we could examine scat and nest-construction, the remains of forbs, bits of hair and fur; if we were particularly lucky or patient we might see the other members of this particular nuclear family, or even the larger clan, if there is a greater neighborhood tribe; but still we would know only a shard of their lives, though they live five feet from the fence, ten feet from the picnic table, fifteen feet from the porch from which launched the death of this particular infant rabbit.

Will we bury it? Yes. Though we could eat it—rabbits are delicious. Yes, I am just kidding. There's not enough meat on it to bother with the meticulous surgery. No, we will not let the dog eat it. Though we should by rights allow the dog to eat it— it's his kill, after all. In the ancient manner he who kills earns the body of the deceased. Thus Achilles and Hector at the gates of Troy. Who was Achilles? He was... I'll tell you that story later. No, we will not let the dog eat the rabbit. We will bury the rabbit out of some inchoate respect. A gesture of reverence, to return to the earth that which essentially arose from the earth. The mother and father rabbit ate what grew from the earth, drank the water that courses through the earth, and that nutrition formed their bodies, from which came this rabbit, who in a real sense is composed of grass and forbs and flowers and clover and bark and buds and rainwater and spring seep and sunlight and mud. One death among many this hour in this yard alone let alone the wide world and perhaps a million other worlds, for all we know. Yes, there could be a rabbit planet. That is not by any means impossible. Could there be a planet where rabbits eat dogs? Yes. Anyone who says something is not possible is arrogant. The only thing you can be sure of is that forms change but energy persists; so it is that you may indeed become a rabbit, a dog, a blackberry bush, a father weeping on the battlements of the walls of a city besieged, a father sitting on the porch muddled and moved at the inquisitive pained faces of his children as they huddle around a torn tiny rabbit, and dig a hole outside the fence, and return the rabbit to the earth from whence it came; and so amen.

Because It's Hard

I was in a monastery the other day and got to talking to a monk who, when I asked him why he was a monk, why he volunteered for a job liable to loneliness, a commitment to an idea no one can ever prove or document, a task that entails years of labor in the belief that somehow washing dishes and cutting grass and listening to pain and chanting in chapel matters in the long scheme of things, said, because it's hard.

I was startled; sure I was. You would be, too. Rarely do people say with a grin that they do something because it hard to do it. But he said it again, still smiling, and then he talked about it for a while, haltingly at first, as he felt for the words, and then with a lovely flow, like something let loose from a dam after a long time pooling behind the dam.

Because I am not sure I can do it at all, let alone do it well, and do it for years and years, perhaps for my whole life, he said. I cannot think that way. I try to be a good monk for a week at a time. Walking helps greatly, I find. Also birds. We have a resident heron here who has been a great help to me. Sometimes he or she is right there by the reeds when I am in pressing need of a heron. I have come to think that the birds are shards of faith themselves in mysterious ways. You could spend a whole life contemplating birds and never come to the end of the amazing things they do. There are many swallows here and I spend hours at a time watching them conduct their intricate maneuvers. They have the loveliest gentle chitter with which they speak to each other in the air. Remarkable creatures altogether. When I was first a monk I was of a mind to adopt one as a pet, and I actually got a ladder and climbed to one of their nests, but when I loomed into view there, surely a great horror to the parents and the young ones, I could not find it in myself to reach in and steal a child. I went back down the ladder and went to the chapel.

I want to be a monk because I think that would be a very good use of me, he continued. Does that sound strange? It sounds a bit arrogant, I suppose. I don't mean to be arrogant. I want to be an implement. Something like a shovel with a beard. If I live with humility and intent, if I do what I do well and grace-fully, that is good. Beyond that I cannot go. When I speak to children they will ask me things like, if I do enough good, and other people do good, then the good stacks up, right? and the good eventually beats the bad, right? and I cannot say this is so. I am not very interested in speculation about such things. I was never interested in theology. I think theology is an attempt to make sense of that to which sense does not apply. I cannot explain why I hope that what I do matters; all I can do is do what I do, either well or ill, patiently or not, gracefully or not. And I do find that doing things mindfully, patiently, easefully, makes the task far more interesting. I love to cut the grass here, for I sometimes come to a sort of understanding with the grass, and the hill, and the creatures in the grass, and with my legs and arms and back, a sort of silent conversation in which we all communicate easily and thoroughly. Do you have any idea of what I mean with all this?

I think I do, I said. I have children and a fascinating graceful mysterious wife and sometimes we are like five fingers in a hand. And sometimes when I write, that happens, that the page and my fingers and my dreams are all the same thing for an hour. I always emerge startled.

Yes, he said, yes, *that* is why I am a monk. I thought perhaps I could add to that larger music, by being a monk. I might have held almost any job, I suppose, been any sort of man—I was very lucky in life, and had a wonderful childhood, and education, and I loved women, and they loved me, and I might have been happy and fulfilled in a dozen ways. But I knew inside that I had to try to do what was hard for me to do, to be of best use.

That's well said, I said.

Then perhaps I was a good monk during the saying of it, he said, smiling again. And now I must be off. Perhaps my best use for the last few minutes was to talk to you; and now my work is certainly to clean the kitchen, for it is Wednesday, and it is my job to make the kitchen shine. Come down a little early tomorrow, before everyone else is up, and see if I have been a good monk for the next couple of hours. Sleep well. The birds begin to sing at about four in the morning. It is my belief that the warblers are first but I could be wrong. A better monk would know, but I am not yet a good monk in that area, though I have hopes.

Were You Lonely When
You Were a Freshman?

A boy asks me, Were you lonely when you were a freshman?, and suddenly there I am again in the bottom bunk of my small room in the old hall, with my roommate snoring above me, the roommate I hardly saw and hardly knew, and when we did talk we could hardly find any common ideas where we could stand together for a moment; thank God for basketball, a language we both did speak, or I might have spent an entire year saying no more than *hey* and *see you later* to that boy; a boy who like so many boys was so shy that he was loud and florid and extravagant and dramatic, to prove that he was anything but shy; that is the way of boys, and probably always has been; and I have known several men who never were able to stop being that boy, it grieves me to say.

Was I lonely when I was a freshman? Yes, for a while, for a time, most of the time, early on; and then I was lucky to find boys whose humor fit my humor, whose smiles were genuine, who didn't mind when I slouched into their rooms to try to fit into my new life somehow; and then somehow one or two began to walk to class with me, and two or three seemed to eat at about the same time that I seemed to eat, so we began to claim a corner table, and so I had a target, in the dining hall, to aim at across the sea of seething laughing burbling students who already fit in, somehow, in ways that I did not yet understand.

And there was always basketball, thank God for basketball, because you could play a game and say *good game* and shake hands and the next time you saw that guy he would say *hey* and maybe pick you for his team and then you would meet other guys with whom to say *hey* and *good game* and *let's play tomorrow at four.*

And I got a job washing dishes, which meant more boys and girls to say hey to, and they would nod and smile and say things like *hey can you cover for me tomorrow* and *hey we are having a party after the game*; and then here and there the same thing happened after classes, boys and girls saying *hey* and *listen we are studying together tomorrow you in?*

And then finally there was a night when my roommate was snoring above me and I lay awake and realized that lonely was gone, that it had ebbed away when I wasn't looking, that it had been crowded out by other people—boys and girls, I began to sense dimly, who had been, every one of them, just as afraid of being lonely as I was, in those first weeks of school. And for the first time in my whole life, I think, I understood that there were no cool kids, no confident kids, no cocky and arrogant buffoons; there were only kids afraid of being lonely, performing and capering in all sorts of ways in order to pretend that they were not; and I began to sense that whatever it is we mean when we use the word *maturity* probably means the moment, if it ever comes, when you finally tire of capering and performing, and stop doing so.

Was I lonely when I was a freshman? Dear yes, heavens yes, inarguably yes; but I do not think that I have ever truly been lonely since, because I finally understood that everyone else was afraid of being lonely, too; and once you understand that, you can try to speak all the languages that people are, behind their masks and disguises and performances. The work of a lifetime, certainly; and maybe, if there is a merciful providence that is entertained by the creative strivings of human beings, more than one, maybe far more than one, maybe only one eternal one, spoken in chapters, as you would tell one story per night to a sleepy child.

Death of a Velociraptor

In today's news, the House Wolf, ever enterprising and relentless when it comes to capturing and dismembering smaller animals in his jurisdiction, leapt off the porch this morning, with that sudden terrifyingly silent ferocious catapult thing that he does, and in two long strides was chewing something to death in the grass. All this happened much faster than that sentence took to write or read. I stood there with the coffeepot, appalled and impressed and curious and empathetic to the victim (do we not all secretly fear sudden wrenching death arriving without warning?), and hoping it was not another wood rat, which would mean I would have to roust out a son to bury the poor shredded thing before some other people in the house saw it.

But it was not a wood rat, though he has killed several wood rats, nor was it a mole, though he has killed several moles, nor was it a red squirrel or a fox squirrel or a gray squirrel, although he has made hay and wreaked havoc among the squirrel communities more than any other single populace, nor was it a crow or jay or wren or sparrow or junco or towhee, though he has made lazy murderous gestures toward all of those. Nor was it a shrew, although I have no doubt that he would kill and eat a shrew, nor a fox or raccoon or even a coyote, all of which I would bet serious money would lose a battle against the House Wolf. No, it was, of all the creatures I did not expect to see dismembered in the grass, a dinosaur.

Now, it was a small dinosaur, as dinosaurs go, although surely it was the case when dinosaurs flourished that the vast majority were small, and lived in the underbrush, and took refuge in the jungles of fern as tall in some cases as today's smaller trees; and it was plastic, which probably most dinosaurs were not, in the years when dinosaurs flourished, long years before there were such things as dogs, or children; and it was, or had been before it was dismembered, a beloved companion for one or both of the boys now sleeping in the house; but those boys were now twenty years old, and more absorbed by girls and cars and final examinations than by small dinosaurs, though there *was* a time when they were totally absorbed by dinosaurs, and by plastic astronauts, and small green soldiers, and imaginative figurines of every sort and shape and stripe, and they played with them for hours at a time, inventing stories as they went, long intricate narratives that I used to sit and listen to with something like awe, that my own small sons were so amazingly inventive, so capable of swift literature and color commentary, so open to story, so quick to explain, with their young tongues, what their restless and curious hands were about, the deft joy of their wizardly hands instantly suggesting a story to their loose and limber brains; and I found, as I stood there on the porch with the coffee pot, staring at the shards of their old friend the green plastic velociraptor, that I missed those hours, when they sprawled on the floor, and I sprawled in a chair pretending to read, or pay the bills, or watch the game, but actually listening, with amazement and affection, as my sons wrote the world under their hands, and spoke the stories aloud with a light and liquid glee.

Angeline

In the last few years before my lovely bride's aged mother died, she lived in a small apartment in a castle for elderly people in gently failing health, and I would visit her there almost every Saturday afternoon, not from a sense of duty but because I liked her wit and erudition and masterful passive-aggression, which was so layered and subtle that I found myself enjoying it immensely as a form of verbal art. There are a lot of ways to be an artist and one way is to be brilliant at saying things which mean the opposite of what you said.

I would knock on her door, even if it was slightly ajar, as it usually was, for she loved to be aware of the passing parade, and she would weakly bid me to enter, and I would shuffle in and announce cheerfully that I could only stay a few minutes, which was my opening salvo, and then we would begin a sort of conversational chess game, during which I would ask after her health, and she would say she felt well, and I would say that means everything hurts, and she would say well not *everything*, and then we would happily discuss her lengthy litany of ills and aches, and compare notes on what parts of our ships were breaking down in the most shocking and offensive manner, such that if you had bought them at a store you would be entitled to triple your money back given the egregious rate of decomposition and shoddy workmanship.

As soon as she said the word workmanship I would pounce, and accuse her of insulting the Force that started the universe into being, and she would pretend to be shocked at my insinuation, and then she would ask me innocently about my Mass attendance, and I would ask her innocently about the various boyfriends she had before she met her beloved late husband, and how many times exactly had she kissed each one and where the nefarious deed was done, and she would giggle in the helpless infectious way a four-year-old giggles, and we would switch to literature, but not before she made the ritual offer to get up and make me tea, which I ritually declined, but knew to be a signal for me to get up and get her a cookie from the blue cookie jar, which she really ought *not* to have, she would say, because I am so fat, and I have decided that today is the day I will go for a long walk, definitely this will happen today, perhaps right after you leave so soon, you must be so very busy to have to rush off like this each time, I am so impressed at how you manage to find time to visit a poor old lady, how very kind of you.

She never went for that walk, of course, never; and it took me a few visits to realize that she did not really want me to stay longer, for that would reduce and dilute the pleasurable pitch of our brief amused play for two actors; and after we talked books for a few minutes (and here she had me, for she was the sort of reader who had read all of Trollope and remembered it too, which is a remarkable sort of reader, but she had a weakness for lesser poetry, which I exploited if I felt she had me on the ropes, she would be questioning me closely about Edward Gibbon and I would innocently mention Ella Wheeler Wilcox or Alfred Marmaduke Hobby and ask why her beloved 19th-century poets had to have three names, what was the deal there? and she would giggle (that great giggle again), then it was time for me to go.

I would rise and she would not, for she was old and she lived in that soft throne of a reading chair, and I would reach down and cup her face for an instant, as a form of hug or kiss, and then I would go, and we would banter as I went, for banter was our language, a way to say things without saying them; and this Saturday morning, like many other Saturday mornings since she died, I miss that. As I got to the door I would ask if she wanted another cookie and she would say I am so fat! and every once in a while now I really want to hear her voice in the next room saying just exactly that.

The Way We Do Not Say What We Mean
When We Say What We Say

O f late I have been ever more absorbed by the way we do not say what we mean when we say what we say; we use all sorts of codes and keys, hints and intimations, signs and signals, to such a degree that even the most blunt and terse remarks, such as *yes* and *no*, quite often do not at all mean affirmation or negation, but rather suggest routes of negotiation, or carry loaded messages having to do with past events and discussions, or are comments on matters of a wholly different import than the one at hand; so that, for example, a quiet *no* means one thing and a loud one another, and a muttered *yes* one thing and a whispered one another, and so on in that vein; and this is not even to enter into conversation about body language, and facial expression, and eyebrow elevation, and percentage of pique, and amount of amusement, or the way that some men, and it seems to be mostly men who do this, pretend to be hard of hearing when they hear something they do not want to hear or respond to or be lured into; so that pretending to be hard of hearing turns out to sometimes be a way of saying something without having to use words, which are so very often misconstrued, misapprehended, misused, or miserable altogether.

We say yes when we mean *I would rather not.* We say no when we mean *I would say yes except for all the times yes has proven to be a terrible idea.* We say no thank you when every fiber in our bodies is moaning *o yes please.* We say *you cannot* when what we mean is *actually you can but you sure by God ought not to.* We say no by staring directly at the questioner and not saying anything whatsoever. We can ask questions that way also.

I am fascinated by how language is a verb and not a noun. I am riveted by how language is a process and not a preserve. I am absorbed by the way that we all speak one language but use different tones and shades and volumes and timbres and pronunciations and emphases in order to bend the language in as many ways as there are speakers of the language. Perhaps every one of us speaks a slightly different language even as we seem to be using the same words to each other. Perhaps all languages are like this although I only know the one language, and that one not so well even after many years or swimming and thrashing and singing in it ever since I was two and three and learning to make sounds that turned people around in the kitchen and made them laugh or occasioned sandwiches and kisses or sent me to my room, ever since I was four and five and learning to pick out letters and gather them together in gaggles and march them in parades and enjoy them spilling down pages and into my fervent dreams.

Perhaps languages use us in ways that we are not especially aware of; perhaps languages are aware that they need us to speak them, or else they go flailing into the dark to be forgotten except perhaps by stones and the oldest of trees. Perhaps languages invent themselves and then have to hunt for speakers. Perhaps all languages began from the music of insects and animals and wind through vegetative creatures. Perhaps languages began with the sound of creeks and rivers and the crash of surf and the whisper of tides, and even now, all these years later, when we open our mouths to speak, out comes not so much meaning and sense and reason and clarity but something of the wild world beyond our deepest understanding. Perhaps much of the reason we so often do not say what we mean to say is because we cannot; there is wild in us yet, and in every word and sentence and speech there is still the seethe of the sea, from whence we came, unto which we will return, which cannot ever be fully be trammeled or corralled or parsed, no matter how hard we try to mean what we say when we say what we think we mean.

The Children of Sandler O'Neill

On the morning of September 11, 2001, eighty-three employees of the investment banking firm Sandler O'Neill & Partners were in the company's office on the 104th floor of the World Trade Center's south tower. Sixty-six of those men and women were murdered by terrorists who smashed a hijacked jet into the tower and caused it to collapse. Those sixty-six men and women, among them, had seventy-six children.

In the harrowing days after September 11, the surviving partners at Sandler O'Neill made several interesting decisions. Some of those decisions had to do with resurrecting the firm, out of rage and duty and defiance, and maybe somehow quietly a sense of ferocious indefatigable unquenchable prayer. Some others of those decisions had to do with the families of the murdered employees: those employees were paid their full salaries, including bonuses, through the end of the year, even though they were deceased; and their families were kept on full employee benefits for the next ten years, even though the employee of record had been murdered; and the firm helped set up a foundation to pay for college for all the children of their murdered employees.

This last decision fascinates and rivets and moves me, and I called the Sandler O'Neill Foundation the other day to talk about those children, and here are some things you should know: fifty-four young men and women have had their college tuitions paid so far, with twenty-two young men and women still eligible for free college tuition. The fifty-four who are attending or have attended college have gone to every shape and sort and stripe of college you can imagine, from Stanford and Princeton and Yale to community colleges and technical institutes to Fordham and Notre Dame and Georgetown. Four students have attended Boston College, the alma mater of Welles Crowther, the twenty-four-year-old Sandler O'Neill employee who saved eleven people from death in the South Tower before running back upstairs to save more people and never being seen again.

The oldest child eligible is now thirty years old and the youngest is thirteen. This youngest child was born six weeks after September 11, 2001. When that child graduates from college, the Sandler O'Neill Foundation will cease to exist, except in memory; but what a resounding memory it will be.

Andy Armstrong is one of the four people who now manage the Foundation; he was one of the founders, in the first days after September 11, though he did not work for or with Sandler O'Neill. He was a friend of Sandler's surviving partner, Jimmy Dunne, and he and many others of Dunne's friends and colleagues and competitors helped set up the Foundation. "We were up and running by the end of the first week after the murders," he says. "We wanted the survivors and their families and the families of the lost to know that we would always remember, that the passing years would never sweep this under the rug. Many dozens of people donated many millions of dollars to set up the Foundation. We have no salaries and no expenses except fees to stay extant. Yes, I know most of the children who went to college. You wouldn't believe some of the letters they have written in appreciation. I think they particularly appreciate that we remember their mom or dad this way. Many of them hardly knew their moms and dads."

I called Jimmy Dunne at Sandler O'Neill to ask him why he instantly did so very much the right thing, the generous thing, the extraordinary thing, when it would have been so easy and normal and understandable to just do enough.

"Because there was a moment in time to stand up," he says, bluntly. "Because we believed at that moment that what happens from now will echo for a hundred years in the families of our people, their kids and their grandkids. Because I knew that how we conducted ourselves in those first few hours and days would define who we really were and what we were about. Because I knew this was the critical hour, and if we just got by without being honorable, then we stood for nothing. I remember staring at the television on September 11, and seeing bin Laden's smirking face, and concluding immediately and irrevocably that we would *not* be intimidated, we would *not* go out of business, we would *not* take our money and run, but that instead we *will* survive, and come back stronger than ever, and flourish, and be an example of people who worked and lived with honor. And that meant taking care of our people and their children with respect and reverence. So we did that.

"We made two key decisions within those first few hours," he says. "One, we would always try to think 'what would bin Laden want?' and then do completely the opposite. He wanted to murder us, and scare us, and make us run and hide, so we would do the exact opposite, and bring the company back better than ever. And two, we would not only flourish, but we would do so the right way. We figured what we did and how we did it was our way of fighting idiots like bin Laden. You want us to fall apart? Then we will survive and flourish. You want to destroy us? Then we will insist even more on acting with honor. That's what the Foundation was for, is for. We want our defiance and reverence to echo for a century, so that the grandchildren of our people will know we stood for something, and acted honorably when it really counted."

Notes from a Wedding

S pent all day and deep into the evening Saturday studying the ways and means and manners by which people gently touch each other, and so communicate this and that and the other thing; to wit,

how fathers gently affectionately lay their hands on the thin eager elegant swannish necks of their children, as a way to say *stay* or *pause here* or *hang on one minute while I complete this conversational business up here and then you can launch off into the distance*;

and the way a man will almost unconsciously but not quite extend his elbow toward the woman he likes best, thus creating a space for her to slip her arm into his as they step through the door or start down the stairs or stroll away from the car toward the event at hand;

and the way that a woman will ever so gently touch the elbow of an older woman (often, it seemed to me, her mother or aunt or grandmother or beloved teacher or nun or neighbor) and so offer support if necessary, or, in one case, steer the older woman toward a room where she might find sunshine and wine;

and the way a man will very briefly touch the shoulder of another man as a way to say hello or goodbye without all the florid folderol of hugging or the formality of shaking hands or the young man's soul-brother gestures and grips and rituals, which turn out to have an expiration date probably sometime in your thirties, after which you turn to the ancient gesture of a gentle touch on the shoulder as a gesture of respect and affection, although there is always one guy who is still into bear-hugs, and another guy who is still into the soul-brother grip, although that latter guy also still has a soul patch, which no man should have past the age of forty, unless he is in a jazz band and can prove it with an unexpired musicians' union card;

and the way young women will artlessly happily joyously unselfconsciously kiss each other on the lips without the slightest care for who thinks what about what in other contexts would seem to indicate romantic interest but which in their cases indicates a cheerful airy unadorned affection for their friends and sisters and cousins and old roommates and fellow members of the musicians' union;

and the way that very elderly men and women will, without the slightest discomfort, hold hands, often both hands, with every single person who stands next to them and talks to them and listens to them, and the first time I noticed this I thought maybe it was for personal safety and security reasons, like being worried about toppling, but the more I noticed it the more it seemed to me that very elderly men and women have stripped away all self-consciousness and worry about what other people might think, and they take a deep honest genuine pleasure in touching their fellow beings, and being touched, and they know better than anyone else how ancient and holy and moving it is to touch and be touched, and they are going to touch and be touched as much as possible in the time granted them to touch and be touched; which seemed to me, as I strolled away from the wedding reception late that evening, arm in arm with the woman I like best, immensely wise, and something to aspire to, perhaps even today, perhaps as soon as you finish reading these words.

The Hills and Dales of Their Father

What was it like to have twin infants?, a student asks, and immediately it is some years ago, on Saturday morning, and my wife and I have taken turns rocking the boys back to sleep during the night, and finally at dawn she carted them both into our big bed, and they fell asleep on me, and she said, firmly, if you move one inch in any direction and wake them up I will never kiss you with arrowed intent again the rest of our lives, and she promptly fell asleep, so there I was, with two boys, age one year each, sprawled on me like moist puppies, like tiny tender shirts, like rumpled drooling bundles of the warmest softest possible cotton.

One of them was draped over my shoulder and was breathing gently and wetly into my ear. The other one was straddling the equator not unlike a belt wearing pajamas. My wife slept deeply. I was not very bitter that she was sleeping deeply and I was forbidden to move under any circumstances whatsoever or else. The thought occurred to me that perhaps the boys were into their own deepest sleep cycle now and I would be unable to move for the next six hours. I had mixed feelings about this. For them to sleep six straight hours would be a miracle beyond the feeble comprehension of any reader who has not survived the first year of an infant's life, during which the parents do not *ever* sleep more than two hours consecutively, and they, the parents, become so addled and muddled with sleeplessness that they lurch around the house like primary voters, mumbling incoherently and eating napkin-and-cheese sandwiches and falling asleep in the shower. On the other hand, if they slept for six hours I would have to be motionless for six hours, and while I *could* wriggle out from under them, and get up gently, and sneak a shower and a napkin sandwich, and hope that a merciful and understanding Proximate Cause would let the boys roll into the warm cave of the blankets and snore back toward their mother like salmon returning to their native waters, the chances of them not waking and wailing were miniscule, and the thought of never being kissed again with serious intent by this particular woman was horrifying, so I stayed motionless.

Even though I have spent many years trying to find the right words to evoke and hint at the extraordinary of the ordinary, I don't think I can adequately articulate how glorious it was to wear not one but two small sleeping sons at dawn on a Saturday while an astounding woman slept like a rock to starboard. Our sons slept with their mouths open slightly. Their hair was discombobulated. Their scent was some combination of moist and pears and toast. One had an arm flung behind him at an impossible angle unless you are one year old and made of whatever substance it is that allows you to put your foot on your head for laughs. The other one, the drooler, was perched in such a way on my shoulder that the thin silver creek of his drool wandered slowly and cautiously around my ramparts, for all the world like it was afraid of something, and was pausing regularly for reconnaissance, and to check the wind.

In *my* memory I was in this motionless state, covered with sons, for several weeks, but my wife says this is not so, and in fact *I* fell asleep, and was snoring like a bear with a deviated septum, and *she* woke up, and took the boys off to be bathed and fed, while *I* slept for another few hours, but this is the most arrant airy nonsense, and I don't remember it that way at all. I do, however, remember how holy and moving it was to have not one but two infant sons asleep on the hills and dales of their father. I don't think I will ever forget that, as long as I live.

On the Bus

Here's a story for you. Here's a story that you will think about the rest of the day. The driver of a school bus tells it to me. He is a big guy who used to be a store detective and soldier when he was young so he sees things. He loves kids so he figured he would close out his earning years driving the local school bus. He's good with his hands and can fix things if need be and he knows basic first aid so he can deal with sick kids if need be and he doesn't mind driving twice a day in the city.

Better me than someone who doesn't like driving, he says.

On his bus, he says, there were usually twenty kids or so. I know every one of them, sure. We have a little chat on the first few days we are together and that establishes the basic rules of the bus. I am not the king of the bus. I am not much for tin-pot dictators. I have seen enough pompous authority in life not to want to add more to the manure pile. So I try to establish basic rules of safety and civility and then leave them pretty much alone. Most of the time this works fine and usually the older kids are sort of casually in charge of the bus. Most of the time everything is fine but sometimes some kids gang up on some other kids. Sure, I notice when that happens. You would be surprised how much you notice even when you are facing the other direction and focused on traffic. Usually I wait a couple of days for it to sort out on its own and usually that happens without fanfare. Kids live intense lives, way more than adults remember. When we get to be older we forget how intense it was being a kid.

One day a new kid joins the bus. His family just moved to town and he's the new kid. He's a big kid, and he's sensitive about that, and he's sensitive about being the new kid, and like anyone who is real sensitive about something he's real prickly about any hint of anyone saying anything about it or even *hinting* anywhere near it. You know what I mean.

So he thinks one of the little kids said something, and he gets in the little kid's face, yelling and stabbing his finger in the little kid's face, and the little kid understandably starts to cry, and I hear all this from the front of the bus, and as this is beyond the rules of safety and civility, I pull the bus to the side of the road, but then something happens. Another little kid inserts himself between the big kid and the little kid. This second little kid is maybe seven years old and the skinniest scrawniest geekiest kid you ever saw but he does what he does, and then another little kid steps in, and another, and then a whole bunch of kids, big and little, surround the little kid, who is still crying. But no one says anything, that's the thing. No one said a word. No one pushes or shoves or anything. They just surround the little kid until he stops crying. The new kid got the message and he sat down and didn't say anything. After a couple of minutes all the kids who had stood up out of their seats against the rules sat back down in their seats, and I got the bus back into traffic and we proceeded on without further incident. So that's all I wanted to tell you, about the other kids getting up one by one and inserting themselves between the little kid and the big kid. Somehow that's a big story, isn't it? And I bet there are a thousand stories a day like that. A million. Probably a billion. Every day. Everywhere. That's something to think about, isn't it? That's something to think about.

Hawk Words

The last time I saw my brother Kevin in the flesh was three years ago, in his den, in the evening, just before summer began. We sat with our legs sprawled out and talked of hawks and love and pain and Mom and beaches and mathematics and Dad and college and his children and mine and our patient mysterious wives and books and basketball and grace and pain and then hawks again. We were both major serious intent raptor guys, delighted to try to discern the difference between say, a kestrel and a jay, which are about the same size, although one can dismember a mouse in seconds and the other would faint dead away if dismemberment was on the syllabus.

Both of us would happily have studied hawks for the rest of our lives, but the problem was that his life was ending soon, and this was the last evening we would have to talk about love and hawks, and we knew this, so we talked about hawks and love.

In my experience brothers don't often talk bluntly about love, even if you do love each other inarticulately and thoroughly and confusedly, because it's awkward to talk about love that's not romantic. Everyone chatters and sings and gibbers about romantic love, and how it starts and ends and waxes and wanes, but we hardly ever talk about all the other kinds of love, which include affection and respect and reverence, and also brothering, which is rough and complicated. Brothers start out in competition and some never stop. Brothers are like trees that start out adjacent but have to grow apart to eat enough light. Brothers worship each other and break each other's noses, and adore each other and steal from each other, and detest each other even as they sprint to defend each other. It's *very* confusing. If you are very lucky you eventually get to be the same age as your brother or brothers. Eventually the differences between and among you erode and dissolve and the love is left in craggy outcrops where you can sit together with your legs sprawled out.

So we talked about love, but we used hawk words. That's what I wanted to tell you this morning. We talked about how it's awfully hard to tell sharp-shinned hawks apart from Cooper's hawks and who *was* Cooper anyway? We talked about the immeasurably old war between crows and red-tailed hawks, and who started that war, and why, and sure it was about a girl, sure it was. We talked about owls and osprey and eagles and kites and falcons and other raptors too but mostly we talked about hawks because we knew hawks and saw hawks every day and had always both been addled and thrilled by hawks and we always would be, even after one of us was ashes in a stone box under an oak tree. We talked about how one of us promised to stay addled and thrilled by hawks as long as he lived so that both of us would still be delighted by hawks somehow. So it is that now when I see a sharp-shinned hawk sliding sideways through oak branches at supersonic speed in pursuit of a flitter of waxwings, my brother Kevin sees that too, even though the prevailing theory is that he is dead. Often I find myself mumbling *o my gawd did you see that?* and he mutters *what could possibly be cooler than that?* and so somehow we are still sprawled and lucky and it is almost summer and we are talking about love.

What Were Once Pebbles Are Now Cliffs

I am standing in the middle pew, far left side, at Mass. We choose this pew where possible for the light pouring and puddling through the stained-glass windows. The late-morning Mass is best because the sun finally made it over the castlements of the vast hospital up the hill and the sun has a direct irresistible shot at the windows and as my twin sons used to say the sun loooves jumping through the windows and does so with the headlong pleasure of a child.

They used to be small enough to choose different sun-shot colors on the floor and jump from one color to another, my sons. They would do this before Mass and after Mass and occasionally *during* Mass on the way back from being blessed by Father John in the years before their own First Communions. Sometimes they would rustle and fidget impatiently in the pews, and fiddle with missals, and fold the parish newsletter into ships and trumpets, and bang the kneeler up and down, until they were arrested by the wither of the maternal glare, but then came Communion, which meant Father John bending down from his great height like a tree in a storm and blessing them with his hand as big as a hat on their heads. They loved that, and loved whispering loudly *Hi Johnny!* to him, which would make him grin, which they counted as a win, to make the sturdy dignified celebrant grin like a kid *right in the middle of Communion!*

When they were three and four years old they used to stand on the pew next to me and lean on me as if I was a tree and they were birds. Sometimes one would fall asleep and I would sense this through my arm and shoulder so that when I sat down I would be sure to haul the sleeper down safely. Sometimes they would lean hard against me to try to make me grin like Father John grinned during Communion. Once I discovered that they had conspired before Mass to lean on Dad so *hard* that they would *squish Dad!* and he would get six inches taller *right there in the church!*, wouldn't that be funny? Sometimes they would lean against me just from a sheer simple mammalian affection, the wordless pleasure of leaning against someone you love and trust. But always I was bigger and they were smaller, then.

Then came years during which there was no leaning because generally they were leaning away from their parents and from the Church and from authority in all its figments and forms and constitutions, and generally they sat silent and surly and solitary, even during the Sign of Peace, which distressed their parents, which was the point.

But now they are twenty and one is much taller than me and the other is much more muscular. One is lanky and one is sinewy. One is willowy and the other is burly. And recently in Mass I leaned against one and then the other and I was moved, touched, pierced down to the fundaments of my soul. What were once pebbles are now cliffs. They are tall and strong and stalwart and charming and at the Sign of Peace people in all directions reach for them smiling. When I lean against them they do not budge and now I am the one leaning against men whom I love and trust and admire. Sometimes I lean too hard against them on purpose just to make them grin. Sometimes by chance I am the first one back from Communion and I watch as they approach, wading gracefully through the shivered colors of the sun streaming through the windows. Time stutters and reverses and it is always yesterday and today. Maybe the greatest miracle is memory. Think about that this morning, quietly, as you watch the world flitter and tremble and beam.

The Final Frontier

It is the rare soul who remembers particular lines from Scripture for reasons other than professional advancement or private absorption, but I remember even a child being totally riveted by the odder blunter saltier lines in the Greatest Story Ever Told—the ones that made me elbow my wry patient dad, like *be kind to your father even when his mind goes,* or the ones where the Christos isn't so much godlike as he is a rattled guy, such as when he whirls and shouts *who touched my clothes?!,* after he *felt the power leave him,* what a phrase!

And one of those lines for me has always been *blessed are the poor in spirit.* I heard that for the first time as a child, of course, at Mass, late in the morning, drowsing between my alpine dad and willowy mother, in a pew filled with brothers seated with parental buffers so as to reduce fisticuffery, and like everyone else I was puzzled and nonplussed; wasn't the whole point to be *rich* in spirit? How could you be bereft spirit-wise, but get a backstage pass to the Kingdom of Heaven? What was *that* all about? Was that a major serious printer's error no one had noticed all these years? Was it supposed to be *pear* in spirit, or something artsy like that?

Diligent schoolteachers subsequently explained it to me, and my gentle wise parents explained it, and learned university professors explained it, and able scholarly writers explained it, and I got the general idea, that the word *poor* there is better understood as *humble,* but *humble* never really registered for me, because I was not humble, and had no real concept of humble, until my wife married me, which taught me a shocking amount about humility, and then we were graced by children, which taught me a *stunning* amount about humility, and then friends of mine began to wither and shrivel and die in all sorts of ways, including being roasted to death on September 11, and I began, slowly and dimly, to realize that humble was the only finally truly honest way to be, in this life; anything else is ultimately cocky, which is either foolish or a deliberate disguise you refuse to remove, for complicated reasons maybe not even you know.

Of course you do your absolute best to find and hone and wield your divine gifts against the dark. You do your best to reach out tenderly to touch and elevate as many people as you can reach. You bring your naked love and defiant courage and salty grace to bear as much as you can, with all the attentiveness and humor you can muster; this is, after all, a miracle in which we live, and we ought to pay ferocious attention every moment, if possible.

But no, you cannot control anything. You cannot order or command everything. You cannot fix and repair everything. You cannot protect your children from pain and loss and tragedy and illness. You cannot be sure that you will always be married, let alone happily married. You cannot be sure you will always be employed, or healthy, or relatively sane.

All you can do is face the world with quiet grace and hope you make a sliver of difference. Humility does not mean self-abnegation, lassitude, detachment; it's more like a calm recognition that you must trust in that which does not make sense, that which is unreasonable, illogical, silly, ridiculous, crazy by the measure of most of our culture; you must trust that you being a very good you matters somehow. That trying to be an honest and tender parent will echo for centuries through your tribe. That doing your chosen work with creativity and diligence will shiver people far beyond your ken. That being an attentive and generous friend and citizen will somehow matter in the social fabric, save a thread or two from unraveling. And you must do all of this with the sure and certain knowledge that you will never get proper credit for it, at all, one bit, and in fact the vast majority of the things you do right will go utterly unremarked; except, perhaps, in ways we will never know or understand, by the Arab Jew who once shouted about his cloak, and may have been somehow also the One who invented and infuses this universe and probably a million others—not to put a hard number on it or anything.

Humility, the final frontier, as my late brother Kevin used to say. When we are young we build a self, a persona, a story in which to reside, or several selves in succession, or several at once, sometimes; when we are older we take on other roles and personas, other masks and duties; and you and I both know men and women who become trapped in the selves they worked so hard to build, so desperately imprisoned that sometimes they smash their lives simply to escape who they no longer wish to be; but finally, I think, if we are lucky, if we read the book of pain and loss with humility, we realize that we are all broken and small and brief, that none among us is actually rich or famous or more beautiful than another; and then, perhaps, we begin to understand something deep and true finally about humility.

This is what I know: that the small is huge, that the tiny is vast, that pain is part and parcel of the gift of joy, and that there is love, and then there is everything else. You either walk toward love or away from it with every breath you draw. Humility is the road to love. Humility, maybe, *is* love. That could be. *I* wouldn't know; I am a muddle and a conundrum, shuffling slowly along the road, gaping in wonder, trying to just see and say what is, trying to leave shreds and shards of ego along the road like wisps of litter and chaff.

Except Ye See Signs and Wonders

Highlight at church yesterday: a small boy, age four or so, crawling ever so deftly and silently out of the front rows, and getting all the way to the edge of the proscenium, and then getting both arms and one leg up on the ceremonial ledge, before he was hauled back to base, giggling so infectiously that everyone in the front rows and the celebrant started laughing too. Even the piano player was snickering, and she is usually the soul of stern decorum.

That the perambulator had, I kid you not, a bright blue Mohawk haircut, and was wearing blue pajamas with black cowboy boots, added to the pleasure of the moment, because you hardly ever see anyone at church wearing pajamas with cowboy boots, not to mention such a rakish haircut. But it was his giggle that got to me, and has stayed with me happily this morning. His giggles were utterly and completely and totally artless. They were not wry comments, or default nervous tics, or conscious efforts to deflate tension, or even the evidence of skepticism suddenly flushed out into the open, as giggles sometimes are. No: they were pure merriment, and they pealed, they rang, they chimed, they pierced the moment and peeled away the normal for an instant, and everyone burst out laughing, and I am fascinated and moved by this, and wish to explore it a bit with you, because isn't his giggling somehow a more naked holy thing than a church service? Isn't it? Somehow, in ways that are hard to articulate?

Let the children come unto me, for of such is the Kingdom of Heaven, he *said* that, he spoke that clear and adamant and inarguable, with none to gainsay him, and very rarely indeed, I would guess, did he say something he was not sure of with every fiber of his inexplicable being. Of children is heaven, in children is heaven, to be like children is heaven, what could that most mysterious Arab Jew *mean* by this?

Not simplicity, for children are anything but simple, as every parent knows. Not brevity of height or paucity of muscle and money, for we know that might is not at all right, and to be rich is to be penniless in the stuff of holiness; he said that too, blunt and clear as always, and adding the image of moaning camels trying to stuff themselves through the eyes of protesting needles so that we would never forget what he said.

Did he mean because they are artless, and have no agendas, no end games, no filters and disguises, no masks and shields to hide behind? Was he hinting that their unadorned speech and untrammeled curiosity are shining paths for us to return to? Did he mean that all the things we mean by accomplishment, and maturity, and reason, and progress, are actually small niggling things that we must finally shuck and lay aside, in order to again be like children, spiritually open and emotionally naked and constantly liable to giggling?

I think so. I am *not* sure he meant that we should all have blue Mohawks and blue pajamas and black cowboy boots in order to be like unto children, although perhaps he did; you can never be quite sure of his wry wit, and it is entirely possible that the boy I heard yesterday morning was indeed a great sign unto the people, and I am the one chosen to perceive him, and report thereof to you. Who can account the ways of the Lord, who himself came into this world as a rotund child, giggling when his mother and father tickled him, and surely making all and sundry within earshot giggle also? Which in some remarkable and mysterious way he still does; and I report this fact to you, so that we can ponder it the rest of the day, grinning widely at the thought of the Lord of the Starfields with a crisp blue Mohawk and black cowboy boots, giggling to beat the band. Remember: except ye see signs and wonders, ye will not believe.

An Open Letter to Caliph Abu Bakr al-Baghdadi

I will start out politely, with the traditional *As-salaam-u alaykum*, peace be to you, and I will even use the title you have given yourself, and I will try to keep this note brief, for I can only imagine the press of your days, what with trying to manage a nascent state, and a fractious staff, and keeping a wary eye out for the many people who would dearly love to blow you to ragged bits smaller than grains of sand.

So, then, a few points to ponder:

First, you do understand, I hope, that murdering people to get other people to listen to your ideas is poor human resource management. It turns out that people get angry and recalcitrant and obdurate and unwilling to listen when you kill their children and lovers and families and friends. They don't get more malleable. Listen, I am Catholic, and my faith tried the whole terrorism thing, and it didn't work out, and was a tremendous waste of money and time and life. We called it the Crusades. You and many other Muslims are still bitter about the Crusades, and well you should be. But glean the lesson; murder isn't persuasive. Did Muslims listen more assiduously to Catholics during and after the Crusades? No? Consider that.

Second, I remind you that there is not one word in the Qur'an, which you believe to be the revealed Word of the One, or in the hadith (the words of the Prophet, peace be upon him), that says innocents may be murdered. Nowhere is that written. Yet you, like other ostensible leaders of the faith in recent years, have allowed and advocated the murder of innocents. I tell you this: you should fear the loss of your soul even more than the retribution of this world. I will assume you do not fear death, for you and I both believe death is only an abrupt change of form; but I say to you that you lead the faithful astray, and that is a sin; you have been responsible for the death of Muslims, and that is a sin; you have been responsible for the death of innocents, who had done nothing to injure the faith, and that is a sin; and you daily injure and reduce Islam in the eyes of a world that would be far better to be educated in what is merciful and gracious about an ancient and admirable faith.

Third, your use of the word jihad is incorrect and offensive: *jihad al-Saghrir* is, as you know, war against oppression. The Qur'an and the Prophet are clear on its rules: it is to be used only against those who would force Muslims from their faith or drive you from your home; it is limited to combatants, and forbidden against innocents; the Prophet himself commanded that civilians be protected from war; and you are commanded by the Prophet to seek peace at every opportunity. Yet you wage war against innocents; you slaughter civilians of every faith, even your own; and you seek no peace, but only endless war, and power, and land, and slaves. You allow prisoners to be murdered and you allow slaves to be raped. Again I say to you: beware your soul, and the souls of those you purport to lead, for you are breaking the very commandments you say are the blood and bone of your life and nominal state.

Fourth, your fearless warriors in Paris just murdered a girl named Elodie. She was twenty-three years old. She had never done anything to you and yours. Her brother searched through the sea of blood for her. His name is Alexis. He kept calling her cell phone. He says you cannot answer violence with violence. He says you have to find ways to get under the fear and blindness of thugs like those who murdered his sister. He says this as he is preparing for her funeral. I cannot imagine saying such extraordinary things but he said them. He says he is not angry, and that you cannot resist an evil person with evil, but you must try to help them solve their problems and thus prevent more evil. He says he is trying to put himself in your place and feel what you feel, so that you and yours will cease to murder innocents like the sister he loved with all his heart, the sister who was a student, the sister who loved to dance, the sister he will never see again in this form the rest of his life, the sister you allowed to be murdered in a dark room filled with screams.

Here is what I want to say to you: He is a better Muslim than you are, and he is not even Muslim. You have acted badly, and should be ashamed and repentant. If you were really a visionary leader, if you were really a devout follower of the Prophet and of the word of the One, you would kneel in the bloody sand and atone for what you have done, and apologize to those who weep, and then arise and turn all your mind and heart and soul to peace; in so doing you may yet save your soul, and turn the eyes and ears of the world finally to what is great and good in Islam, which is reverence, and purity, and peace.

It is traditional in my culture to end a letter with some expression of regard, but I am not as good a man as young Alexis in Paris, and I will restrain my fury, and conclude only with prayers that you will awake from your squirming darkness, and be, finally, a true Muslim.

A Prayer for You and Yours

Well, my first prayers as a parent were *before* I was a parent, because my slight extraordinary mysterious wife and I had been told by a doctor, bluntly and directly and inarguably, that we would not be graced by children, and I remember us walking out of the doctor's office, silently, hand in hand, and then opening the passenger door to our car for my wife, as my mother had taught all her sons to do or else she, my mom, would reach up and slap you gently on the back of the head for being a boor, and I helped my wife into the car, and bent down to escort the hem of her blue raincoat into the car before closing the door gently, and then I started to walk around to the driver's side, and I burst into tears, and bent over trunk of the car, and sobbed for a moment.

My first prayers as a parent, those tears.

Then we prayed for a long time in all sorts of ways. I prayed in churches and chapels and groves and copses and hilltops and on the rocky beaches of the island where we lived at that time. I would have prayed to all the gods who ever were or ever would be except I know somehow deep in my heart that there is one Breath, one Imagination, one Coherent Mercy, as a friend of mine says, and that everything that is came from and returns to That which we cannot explain or understand, but can only try to perceive the spoor, clues, evidence, effect, the music in and through and under all things.

I have never thought that prayers of request can be answered; I do not think that is the way of the Mercy; yet we do whisper prayers of supplication; I think we always have, since long before our species arrived in this form. Sometimes I think that beings have been praying since there were such things as beings; I suspect all beings of every sort do pause and revere occasionally, and even if we think, with our poor piddly perceptive apparatus, that they are merely reaching for the sun, or drying their wings, or meditating in the subway station between trains, or chalking the lines of a baseball field ever so slowly and meticulously, perhaps they are praying in their own peculiar particular ways; who is to say? Who can define that which is a private message to an Inexplicable Recipient? So that he who says a scrawny plane tree straining for light in a city alley is not a prayer does not know what he is saying, and his words are wind and dust.

* * *

Three children were granted to us, a girl and then, together, one minute apart, two boys; and my prayers doubled, for now I knew fear for them, that they would sicken and die, that they would be torn by dogs and smashed by cars; and I felt even then the shiver of faint trepidation that someday, if they grew up safely, and did not suffer terrible diseases, and they achieved adulthood, that they would be heart-hammered by all sorts of things against which I could not protect or preserve them; and so I did, I admit it, sometimes beg the Coherent Mercy, late at night, for small pains as their lot, for relatively minor disappointments, for love affairs that would break apart but not savagely, for work that they would like and even maybe love. In the end, I remember vividly, I boiled all my prayers as a parent down to this one: Take me instead of them. Load me up instead of them. Let me eat the pains they were served for their tables. I don't think I ever fully understood the deep almost inexplicable love of the Christ for us, why he would accept his own early tortured death as a sacrifice, until I had been a father for a while.

* * *

Somehow being a father also slowly but surely changed the target of my prayers over the years; before we were granted children, I chatted easily and often with my man Yesuah ben Joseph, a skinny gnomic guy like me, a guy with a motley crew of funny brave hard-working bone-headed friends, a guy who liked to wander around outdoors, a guy who delighted in making remarks that were puzzling and memorable and riddlish, a *guy*—I felt like I knew him pretty well, what with us both being guys and all, and I had confided stuff to him not only as a child, but again after the years during which every Catholic boy in my experience ran screaming and shouting away from the Church, away from authority and power and corporate corruption and smug arrogant pompous nominal bosses issuing proclamations and denouncing dissent.

You tiptoe back toward religion, in my experience, cautiously and nervously and more than a little suspicious, quietly hoping that it wasn't all smoke and nonsense, that there is some deep wriggle of genius and poetry and power and wild miracle in it, that it is a language you can use to speak about that for which we have no words; and in my case, as in many others I know, this was so, and I saw for the first time in my life that there were two Catholic Churches, one a noun and the other a verb, one a corporation and the other a wild idea held in the hearts of millions of people who are utterly disinterested in authority and power and rules and regulations, and very interested indeed in finding ways to walk through the bruises of life with grace and humility.

So when I tiptoed back into Catholicism, and began taking it seriously, and began exploring and poking under the corporate hood, curious and fascinated by the revolutionary genius under the Official Parts, it was because I was a father, and knew that I needed a language with which to speak to my children of holiness and prayer and miracle and witness and hope and faith; and I found, month by month as my children grew from squirming lumps to toddlers and willowy young people and now almost men and woman, that it was to her that I turned, both in desperation and in cheerful silent moments when I chanted the Hail Mary to myself while waiting for the coffee to boil.

Why? Because, I think, she was a mother—*is* a mother. He came out of her. That was a miracle. It is a miracle when a child emerges from his or her mother. I had seen this miracle not once but twice, with my own eyes, from very close to the field of action, and I think something awoke in me after that, something that knew she was there, available, approachable, patient, piercing. Not once in the days since my children were born have I ever felt her absence. I do not say this in a metaphorical way, or as a cool literary device, or as a symbolic hint. I mean what I said. I feel her near us. I have no opinion about visitations, other than to grin at the ones where people see her face in tortillas and on stop signs, and to wonder quietly about ones like that which occurred to Juan Diego on the Hill of Tepeyac, long ago, that poor man who had to return to the hill for proof to offer the ecclesiastic authority, who gaped when a shower of roses fell to the shivering floor. Perhaps most reports are hallucinations; perhaps all of them. But perhaps hallucinations are illuminations, and there are countless more things possible than we could ever dream. One thing I know at this age: if you think you know the boundaries and limits and extents of reality, you are a fool. Thus we pray.

* * *

I still pray for them every day. So does my wife, in the morning, by the bed, on her knees, in her pajamas, with her face pressed down upon the blanket of the bed, abashed before the light of the Lord. I have seen this, though I try to be out of the bedroom so that she can pray in private; and every time I see it I get the happy willies, that she believes with such force and humility. But I pray on my feet, by the coffee pot, while walking, while waiting for eyeglasses, while stirring the risotto, while washing the dishes, while brushing my teeth, while scratching the dog. I pray that they will be happy. I pray that they will find work that is play. I pray that their hearts will not be stomped on overmuch—enough to form resilience, but not enough to crush their spirits. I pray that they will live long and be blessed by married love and be graced by children and maybe even grandchildren. I pray that their minds hum and sing and do not stutter and fail. I pray that they will not be savaged by illnesses, but be allowed to live healthy and happy for years beyond my ken and my own life. I still pray to die before they do. I still say thank you, every day, every single day, for being granted children at all; for I am a man who was told, bluntly and directly and inarguably, that my extraordinary bride and I would not be graced by children, and we walked out of the doctor's office, silently, hand in hand, and we wept.

Our first tears as parents.

We have cried many tears since, for many reasons, and our children have been tumultuous, and troubled, and in great danger, and our marriage has been wonderfully confusing, and troubled, and in great danger; but even now, all these years later, every few weeks, I will find myself in tears for what seems like no reason at all; and I know it is because we were blessed with children, three of them, three long wild prayers; and they are the greatest gifts a profligate Mercy ever granted shuffling muddled me. When I am in my last hour, when I am very near death, when I am so soon to change form and travel in unaccountable ways and places, I hope I will be of sound enough mind to murmur this, to our three children, and perhaps, if the Mercy has been especially ridiculously generous, our grandchildren: It was for you that I was here, and for you I prayed every day of your life, and for you I will pray in whatever form I am next to take. Lift the rock, and I am there; cleave the wood, and I am there; call for me, and I will listen; for I hope to be a prayer for you and yours long after I am dust and ash. Amen.

A Note of Thanks

Many of these essays first appeared in *The American Scholar* magazine's lively electric version (theamerican-scholar.org), and I thank my patient editor Sudip Bose there, for the deftest and lightest of editorial touches. My thanks also to my long-suffering editors at *The Christian Century, The Harvard Review, Eureka Street* in Australia (eurekastreet. com.au), *U.S. Catholic, The Timberline Review, Orion, Notre Dame Magazine, St. Anthony Messenger, Brevity, America, Sojourners, The Oregonian, Howl, The Superstition Review,* and *Portland Family.* And my particular thanks to Andrew Snee and Sy Safransky at *The Sun* (a terrific magazine and no mistake, and if you have not seen it you should, thesunmagazine.org), and to Rusty Reno at *First Things.* I think it took some editorial courage and brass to publish "An Open Letter to Caliph Abu Bakr al-Baghdadi," which *First Things* did (occasioning a hilarious endless rabid spitting parade of lunatic responses), to its eternal credit.

—*Brian Doyle*

ABOUT THE AUTHOR

Brian Doyle (born in New York in 1956) was the editor of *Portland Magazine* at the University of Portland, in Oregon. He was the author of many books, among them the novels *Mink River* (set in Oregon), *The Plover* (in the South Seas), *Martin Marten* (on Oregon's Wy'east mountain, foolishly often called Mount Hood), and *Chicago* (take a guess). Among his other books are the story collection *Bin Laden's Bald Spot,* the nonfiction books *The Grail* and *The Wet Engine*, and many books of essays and poems. Brian James Patrick Doyle of New Yawk was cheerfully NOT the great Canadian novelist Brian Doyle, nor the astrophysicist Brian Doyle, nor the former Yankee baseball player Brian Doyle, nor even the terrific actor Brian Doyle-Murray. He was, let's say, the ambling shambling Oregon writer Brian Doyle, and happy to have been so.

Made in the USA
Lexington, KY
19 January 2018